HIGH-LEVEL MANPOWER IN
ECONOMIC DEVELOPMENT
THE TURKISH CASE

———

RICHARD D. ROBINSON

HARVARD MIDDLE EASTERN MONOGRAPH SERIES

HARVARD MIDDLE EASTERN MONOGRAPHS

XVII

HIGH-LEVEL MANPOWER IN ECONOMIC DEVELOPMENT THE TURKISH CASE

BY

RICHARD D. ROBINSON

DISTRIBUTED FOR THE

CENTER FOR MIDDLE EASTERN STUDIES
OF HARVARD UNIVERSITY BY
HARVARD UNIVERSITY PRESS
CAMBRIDGE, MASSACHUSETTS
1967

LIBRARY OF CONGRESS CATALOG CARD NUMBER: 67–25400

PRINTED IN THE UNITED STATES OF AMERICA

TO KIT,
whose process of growing
toward a creative and
constructive adulthood
gave much food for thought
relevant to this little
volume

INTRODUCTION

Human society is evolutionary. It moves forward only so fast as the mind of Man permits. Regardless of the quantity and quality of machines which may be thrust into a given society, that society will fail to reach self-sustaining development if its base of scientific thought and technical knowledge and skill is inadequate, incentives weak, individual vigor lacking, and a sense of common purpose and participation absent. There is little doubt that Turkey, despite the impressive progress made during the republican era, suffers on these counts.

The major bottleneck in Turkish agricultural development continues to be scarcity of enlightened farmers; in industry, of trained management; in business, of qualified executives; in government, of efficient administrators; and in society at large, a paucity of scientific thought, personal initiative, entrepreneurship, and a sense of participating in a common effort toward worthwhile goals.

The authors of Turkey's 1963–1977 development plan and the leaders of contemporary Turkey appear convinced that education in its widest sense must be a basic consideration in the formulation of any long-range economic development or investment program. The fact that input-output relationships in the manpower development sector cannot be quantified easily does not diminish the importance of this sector in planning. It enters importantly into the production function. It should be noted that education can be a means of accelerating human evolution; conversely, it can be the means whereby all forward movement is stopped or even set in reverse. Education *per se* is not enough; content is of vital import, as well as the social context into which it is thrust.

It seems no longer controversial that for modern man basic education must consist largely of training or programming the human mind to think scientifically, that is, to identify problems and to seek optimum solutions within social and physical restraints, restraints which are found in reality and not in emotion or dogma. The mere acquisition of knowledge is not too useful, so rapidly does it expand and change. Only the scientific thinker appreciates this temporal dimension of "truth" and is constantly rethinking his premises and reanalyzing his environment, thereby making possible the application of knowledge to rapidly-changing environmental conditions.

Scientific attitude and manner of thought cannot be taught by the rote learning of a vast amount of miscellaneous and assorted facts generated by past experience. Rather, its prerequisite is veneration of objective evidence, rejection of unreasoned authority, conscious distinction between reason and emotion, separation of logical hypothesis from superstition and prejudice, questioning of the "inevitable," and the singling out of significant relationships. Once the mind learns to follow such channels of thought, knowledge flows. Recent changes in official Turkish educational philosophy indicate that Turkey's educational leaders are moving in this direction.

Conditioning for scientific thought probably begins most effectively at the age of self-consciousness, possibly at the age of two or three. In the absence of such positive early environmental influence and in the presence of distinctly negative ones — as is the case of much Turkish village and lower-class urban society — the job of education (whether civilian or military, whether formal or on-the-job) becomes that much more difficult and important. The first task of the educator then becomes that of opening the mind of the individual to entirely new stimuli and in conditioning his response along unfamiliar lines.

Despite the strenuous effort made under enlightened Turkish leadership, and although this sort of generalization is decreasingly valid, the characteristic Anatolian village family still lives largely in an environment of venerated authority, unquestioned tradition, unchallenged superstition and prejudice, and accepted "inevitability." It is not that the Anatolian is stupid or lazy as some would have it. Scientific evidence leads one to conclude that there are no significant differences in native intelligence among various human types. No doubt, potential Einsteins till the soil of Anatolia with ox and wooden-stick plough. (In fact, a leading nuclear physicist resident in the United States is of Anatolian village origin.) It is rather that the Anatolian is conditioned historically to think in different terms, terms which were perhaps perfectly functional in a pre-Newtonian world but are no longer tenable.

It is those attitudes listed above which the typical Turkish child brings to school or work with him. Education or work experience can either reinforce these attitudes or replace them by scientifically-reasoned thinking. In the former case, self-sustaining development is unlikely — in the latter, probable. Hence, only if education follows the second course does an increasing investment in public education make sense.

Education, of course, represents investment by society in the individual. The target is maximum realization of the individual's potential social value, either as a primary producer of goods and services of value to his fellows or as a catalyst to further production by inducing an increased productivity on the part of others. Thus, the training of a technician is a direct means whereby productivity can be increased; the education of a manager or a teacher is an indirect method (via more efficient organization, and the spread of insight, incentives and skills) toward the same end. All require attention.

Of equal importance is the schooling of the ordinary citizen who is neither master technician nor skilled manager or teacher, but who must actually be all three in terms of maximizing the potential of his own life. Surely, it is only through such general education that an enlightened, progressive, integrated society can evolve. And it is only within such a society that the tools of science can be created, used and controlled to bring about a greater and greater flow of useful goods and services and an ever-increasing standard of living within an increasingly free society, free in the sense of liberating the human spirit from preoccupation with physical constraints or unreasoned tradition.

The mere tools of production are not enough. It is the human element in all productive enterprise which poses those problems most difficult of solution. Everywhere, the primary long-range bottleneck in production and material progress arises out of the shortcomings of the human mind — not in intelligence, but in education, training, and motivation. Superstition, prejudice, ignorance, and unreasoned trial-and-error "thinking" not only are incongruous to science and mechanization but can easily neutralize the social benefits emanating from these processes. One refers here not only to the ruling elite, but also to the ordinary individual — the common man.

Effective use of machines and technology in an increasingly open society is exceedingly improbable in the absence of skilled labor, trained mechanics, professional managers, responsible scientists, effective teachers, and an enlightened public to control the use of those machines for the social good. Creation of a modern, efficient agricultural system is surely unlikely in the absence of literate, progressively-minded farmers who can — or want to — calculate productivity and unit costs and take reasoned steps to improve both. Efficient operation of large-scale industry is equally unlikely in the absence of trained management which can — or wants to — control scientifically the productive process or of an enlightened labor force which exerts constant social and economic pressure on management, but neither too much nor too little. In short, it is impossible to consider any society efficient or productive, i.e., progressive — which is not at all times attempting to make the most of the potentialities of its human resources.

In the twentieth century a national community is only as strong as the body of scientific thought within that community. By this measure, the Turkish national community is still dangerously weak. Regardless of the impressive progress made by Turkey during recent years, its base of scientific knowledge remains small, confined largely to a small group of educated town and city folk. And there is evidence that this city-village disparity is growing. Despite the capital investment in machines and technical skills, this is not the foundation upon which can be constructed a highly productive, efficient, independent nation — and hence, one with a high standard of living for its people, including relative freedom of individual choice in respect to style of living.

In approaching the Turkish problem we should not assume that the institutions, incentives and policies that have been more or less effective in a United States or western European context will prove to be optimum in the Turkish context. As Philip H. Coombs has written so cogently,

Educational development requires reform and innovation as well as quantitative expansion. . . . Expenditures on the wrong kind of education or on highly inefficient educational arrangements can be downright wasteful and even counterproductive. . . . There is great need here for discovery and inventions, and for new internal institutional mechanisms whose function is to help education renew and reform itself. *

As we plunge into the Turkish case, we should erase from our minds any educational or manpower development concepts of the "self-evident truth" variety. What is functional in the United States in the optimum developmental sense may be dysfunctional in Turkey. Specific examples may be, to mention but a few, the ideas of universal literacy, an eleven or twelve-year pre-college education, local responsibility, age-grade levels, Western levels of competence for the award of technical or professional diplomas, the recruitment of students, or the separation of basic education from vocational training. Turkish educators have attempted a number of novel experiments from which all of us can gain insight into the educational process. And they are on the verge of instituting more. It is for these reasons that Turkey deserves the close attention of those concerned with manpower development.

In the writing of this study, I have been greatly aided by the critical reading given to the manuscript by Professors Charles A. Myers and Daniel Lerner of the Massachusetts Institute of Technology, and by William A. Johnson of The Rand Corporation. They are, however, hereby absolved from any responsibility for the shortcomings of this small volume. I wish here to add my thanks to the Inter-University Study of Labor Problems in Economic Development for stimulating this project and making additional field research possible. Finally, I wish to thank Mrs. Brenda Holmes, my faithful assistant in preparing the manuscript for publication.

Cambridge, Massachusetts   R. D. R.
January, 1967

* In his *Education and Foreign Aid* (Cambridge: Harvard University Press, 1965), p. 10.

CONTENTS

LIST OF TABLES

CONTENTS   xiii

LIST OF CHARTS

HIGH-LEVEL MANPOWER IN
ECONOMIC DEVELOPMENT
THE TURKISH CASE

I

THE HISTORICAL INPUT

Excepting a small urban elite, republican Turkey showed little evidence of sustained social, economic or political modernization until the post World War II era. Prior to that time, none of the usual economic indicators had moved up significantly. Nor had the social or political systems seemed to have undergone fundamental change. Some 70 per cent of the people still lived in 40,000 agrarian village communities — semi-isolated, near subsistence, pre-Newtonian, tradition-bound. Another 10 per cent lived in the provincial market towns, also tradition-bound and pre-Newtonian for the most part. The few modernizers in Ankara and Istanbul were virtually isolated from the grass roots. Political practice remained monolithic and authoritarian under the single-party regime headed by a retired army general, first Mustafa Kemal Atatürk, later, Ismet Inönü. Modernization was forced. In fact, however, many unseen forces had coalesced by 1945 to propel Turkey to the brink of a dramatic dynamism which, within a decade and a half thereafter, would breed instability and insecurity in what had hitherto been an enormously stable and secure society.

Turkey's political stability prior to 1950 had probably been a function of uninterrupted independence, which gave the Turks a sense of responsibility, an administrative tradition, and a sense of greatness (a residue of Ottoman status). The momentum of the Atatürk regime, the removal of the capital to an interior provincial seat, the dispersed and isolated nature of the population, the *national* identification of a political elite (rather than identity with a locality and local interests), the subsistence level of living of most Turks, and popular adherence to the "warrior virtues" (among which obedience ranked high) had contributed to this stability.

Events immediately following 1945 tended to erode each of these elements of stability. Turkish independence had been seriously undermined by unprecedented dependence upon the West, and the United States in particular, for military and economic support. Hence, the Turks were beginning to lose their sense of responsibility. Vicious partisan politics had befouled the administration. The memory of Ottoman greatness was fading, and the momentum of Atatürk was dissipating. The capital, Ankara, was no longer an isolated, relatively small town. Indeed, the nation's population had doubled and was beginning to swamp Ankara, Istanbul, and Izmir, thereby subjecting the government to pressure from the streets. The political and bureaucratic elite was demonstrably more local in identity. The standard of living had risen off the subsistence level, and the "warrior virtues" were being challenged by more liberal virtues, plus economic incentive. A very much more fluid situation had developed by, say, 1955.

A significant measure of the change was the dramatic increase in the geographical mobility of the population following World War II. For example, from Table 1, we can derive comparable mobility indices for the years 1938, 1948, and 1955. Note that the index increased by only 20 per cent, from 173 to 208, during the early decade, but from 208 to 521, or by 150 per cent during the next seven years. Correspondingly, the percentage of the population living outside the province of their birthplace steadily pushed upward. The

TABLE 1. MOBILITY OF TURKISH POPULATION

MEASURE	1938	1948	1955
Road, passenger-kilometers	500,000,000#	1,211,070,000	8,090,000,000
Rail, passenger-kilometers	1,185,500,000	2,545,800,000	3,917,300,000
Air* passenger-kilometers	12,000	20,868,000	68,682,000
Sea* passenger-kilometers	253,440,000	389,600,000	428,800,000
TOTAL	2,938,952,000	4,167,338,000	12,504,782,000
Population	17,016,000	20,056,000	24,065,000
Mobility index (total/pop.)	173	208	521

Source: R. D. Robinson, *Developments Respecting Turkey*, vol. IV (New York: American Universities Field Staff, 1957), pp. 244–45.
* Includes some foreign travel.
# No actual data available. Assumed.

figure for 1950 was 8.0 per cent; for 1955, 10.4 per cent; for 1960, 11.4 per cent.[1]

THE POLITICAL AND MILITARY CYCLES

To assess the general impact of any variable introduced into the Turkish picture, such as a manpower development program, it should be superimposed on two interlocking circles of events (diagrammed in Chart I).

To illustrate the dynamics of this system in the Turkish context, a brief survey of recent political and economic history is useful. Taking as a point of departure the regime of the Sultan-Caliph Abdul Hamid II (1876–1909), we should note that although it represented continuing reform and innovation it was progressively less successful in introducing change, and eventually the regime was destroyed by revolution. What the Palace had failed to sense was the interrelationship between modern technology and the nature of social and political institutions. As the traditional political and administrative institutions of the Ottoman Empire became less and less functional for a modernizing society, opposition to the regime grew, an opposition anchored firmly in the skilled elite, first predominantly civilian and later military as well.

CHART I. TURKEY'S MILITARY AND POLITICAL CYCLES

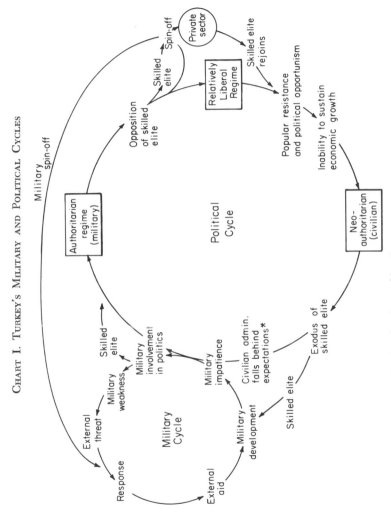

* May be a short-lived, liberally-oriented regime at this point.

Technological development requires increasing participation in the decision-making process by those in command of the technology. A liberalization of political structure is thus dictated to permit that participation. Abdul Hamid responded by instituting more and more political restraints, which was tantamount to making the traditional institutions even more resistant to change. At the same time, the skills which the regime needed to effect desired technological innovation — particularly in the area of military and communications — were being denied it due to the disaffection of a significant portion of the elite. Initially, that part of the skilled elite, largely civilian, committed to Western political ideals — i.e., secularism and liberalism — constituted the alienated group. As the military-political situation deteriorated, the military became involved in politics and provided the activist leadership that the civilian revolutionaries lacked. The 1908 revolution and the installation in 1912 of a military-oriented authoritarian regime followed. It seems quite clear that the political involvement on the part of the military led to a weakening of the latter, examples of which were the politically-motivated opposition of Enver Pasha to Mustafa Kemal Atatürk, Enver's declaration of war against the Allies, and the ill-considered eastern campaign in 1916 on which Enver insisted. Political ideology and personal ambition tend to shield an individual from military reality.

The military weakness of the Turks quickly generated an external threat: the Allied attacks of World War I and the subsequent Allied attempts to occupy virtually all of Anatolia, an attempt spearheaded by the Greek invasion of Anatolia through Izmir in 1919. Through a combination of chance, mistakes on the part of the Allies, and brilliant leadership on the Turkish side, the strength of the Turkish military was regenerated in time to cancel Allied designs on the

Turkish heartland and to wrest a treaty of peace that acknowledged Turkish sovereignty over what constitutes contemporary Turkey, with but minor change. This military response had led to some external assistance from the Soviet Union. Also the all-out national struggle that developed against the invading Christian forces enjoyed the support of the skilled elite.

During the period of consolidation for the new nationalist regime in Ankara, following its defeat of the invaders in 1922, Mustafa Kemal Atatürk gradually drew the strings of political control tighter. The regime became strongly authoritarian under the personal guidance of Atatürk, a military man who was assisted by Ismet Pasha (Inönü), another military man. But the political restraints were used to force the pace of social, political, and technical innovation, Atatürk and his colleagues apparently being aware of interrelationships involved. The civilian administration became attractive to young men of ambition and skill. Meanwhile the army fell more and more into a rigid, Prussian-like caste system, and received a lower and lower proportion of the national resources. At the outbreak of World War II, it was still wearing World War I uniforms, carrying World War I weapons, and committed to World War I tactics. During the interwar period, those with innovating skills were not likely to be attracted by a military career.

When leadership passed from Atatürk to Ismet Inönü, upon the former's death in 1938, much of the dynamism of the earlier period of Atatürk reforms had already slackened. It was evident that Inönü was not the charismatic leader that Atatürk had been. This fact, plus the external threat to Turkey implicit in World War II, led to fairly rigid political restraints. And, once the external threat had passed, a large number of the skilled elite, long restive under Inönü's leadership, moved out of the government into the private sector, either in fact or in spirit. The civilian-led party of free enterprise and political liberalism, the Democrats, won a smashing victory in 1950 in virtually every city and town where this issue was of some relevance. For the mass of voters in the countryside, of course, other issues dominated.

Too much was expected of liberalism and too little was understood of the problems inherent in the process of accelerated national development in which Turkey was now caught up. Basic structural changes were under way, and economic incentives were beginning to penetrate the popular mind for the first time. Perhaps it was inevitable that a critical balance of payments problem and internal inflation should arise. As the government under Prime Minister Adnan Menderes reasserted economic powers so hastily dumped following 1950, the opposition — the party of Atatürk and now of Inönü — opportunistically challenged the government on every move in order to gain political advantage from frustrated popular demand for increased consumption of non-available or increasingly high-priced goods. The regime reacted by asserting political controls, thereby acting contrary to the liberal political convictions of a large percentage of the elite carrying the skills the government needed to organize and manage the economy. Disaffection grew, first civilian and then military.

As has been observed, the military had been virtually abandoned during the interwar period. Then came the threat to Turkey carried by World War II. This threat generated massive external military assistance — first British, German, and French, and then, after 1947, American. This onrush of arms and military skills had the net effect of recreating a dynamic, modernizing military establishment. As a result, a military career became increasingly attractive during the 1945–60 era to ambitious young men who depended on demonstrable skill for social position, i.e., the innovators, particularly those of rural or lower class urban origins to whom other avenues of advancement were closed. As the Menderes regime became bogged down in vicious partisan politics and as economic development slowed, a number of the younger military officers saw the situation as a threat to Turkey's survival as a modernizing state — indeed, perhaps as a state at all. The final result was the May 1960 military coup which ousted the Democrats and set the stage for the second republic.

But opposition on the part of many members of the skilled elite to continued military leadership and to the coalition civilian governments that followed was apparent. A disaffection from the military and from a weak central government took place. More of the elite began to feel that the non-resolution of Turkey's basic social and economic problems was not the fault of any one person or political party, but possibly was due to inconsistencies between economic objectives and political institutions. That is, the objective of long-run economic growth at a rapid (i.e., "catch-up") pace required an optimum allocation of resources. On the other hand, the operation of a free economy, it was suspected, would not bring about such an allocation, for the mass of consumers were concerned only with immediate consumption. Therefore, what one sees in Turkey as of this writing is growing support by the skilled elite for the idea of a strong central government committed to essentially socialist concepts. The reason it is so difficult to identify the leading political parties in Turkey as being on the right or left — as rated by the degree of government control over the economy each proposes — is that the elite in each case is really socialistic but finds itself required to compete for the popular vote on the basis of immediate consumption. One suspects that if any party can maintain a clear working majority, political restraints will be reimposed so that a number of unpopular moves may be undertaken — e.g., tax reform, land consolidation, holding the line on consumption, etc. If such moves are undertaken ostensibly as part of a modern social welfare economic planning effort, a large part of the skilled elite will possibly cooperate, for much faith has been lost in liberal economic policies. Even the leading private industrialist in the country is quoted as having declared that the government should somehow lure or compel industry to locate in the less-developed parts of the country.

Therefore, perhaps the "private sector" shown in Chart I should now be reconstructed as the socialist sector of a third cycle, one of economic ideology. In fact, we are indeed speaking of a cycle, for as the economy becomes more and more complex in terms of the decisions required, central planning becomes increasingly onerous and is likely to generate its own opposition, which we now see in some of the more advanced socialist countries. The point is that the entire system is highly unstable so long as (1) a significant number of the skilled elite is committed to liberal political ideals, (2) the rural masses continue to demand the right to immediate consumption of gains in productivity, (3) the military feels obliged to take over political functions whenever the civilian administration falters. Behind these pressures is the basic conflict between the commitment by both the military and civilian elites to accelerate the national development at a "catch-up rate" (officially defined as a 7 per cent annual increase in Gross National Product) and the compelling desire felt by the mass of Turks — newly risen off the subsistence level — to consume, rather than to save and invest in the tools of future production, that is, in sustained economic growth. But if the skilled elite reshapes its liberal ideology, a rapprochement between civilian and military elite may be possible, in which case popular demand for immediate consumption may be ignored for a time. An alternative is an increasingly brittle political situation as new class-identified political parties appear.

It is apparent that after a decade of relatively liberal multi-party government, capped by a military coup d'état, the introduction in 1961 of competent economic planning into the Turkish picture did not produce the stability expected by some. The problem of Prime Minister Adnan Menderes' regime, which had held power from the 1950 general election to the 1960 coup, was not so much the misallocation of resources — assuming a growth maximization calculus — as its inability to gain political acceptance for the moves necessary to institute such optimum allocation. There is little point to economic plans if the state cannot capture the resources for their implementation or if the flow of transfer payments within the economy (i.e., taxes, subsidies, etc.) — seen initially as a stimulant to growth in the villages — cannot be shifted so as to coincide with the changing requirements for sustained growth. The post-1960 regime has drawn up an apparently well-conceived plan, but has not solved the political problems inherent in its implementation. Nor has the Justice Party, which secured a parliamentary majority in the October 1965 general elections, resolved these problems.

CLASS ROLES AND SOCIAL CHANGE

These movements around the political and military cycles may be viewed as socially horizontal in their main thrust. Meanwhile, along a vertical axis, another dynamic sociopolitical process is undoubtedly taking place as class identities of various groups shift. The only meaningful distinction that occurs to an observer who differentiates various socioeconomic strata lies in the manner in which members of a given stratum react to the social structure. That is, to what extent is the social structure seen as satisfying their needs?

This assumes that those on a particular level react similarly, but differently from those on another level — which is a very large assumption as we shall see. These levels, incidentally, we can define operationally in terms of relative income: in Turkish cities, the middle-class range would be say from about 1,200 to perhaps 3,000 Turkish lira; in smaller places, 800 to 1,800 Turkish lira. We use income because it is a rough measure of authority, admittedly even rougher for a semi-cash, relatively traditional society (as Turkey) than for a full fledged market-oriented, modern society. What we would really like to get at in determining class identity is the circle of individual influence. This can be done indirectly by measuring an individual's command over wealth and income, which in turn tends to be associated with certain roles to which society assigns relative values.

For example, a member of the middle class may expect realistically to satisfy in large measure his economic and social expectations within the existing social structure. It is often argued that given the dynamics of the social system, he can reasonably expect that either he, himself, or his children will move into the upper class without a major change in the social system. Indeed, a major change in the social system would be seen as blocking such a realization, hence the tradition of middle class conservatism and political stability. The social-psychological investment in rising to upper-middle-class status represents a vested interest in the existing structure, in that the return on that investment will be realized fully only in the future when the individual or his scion moves into the upper class. That day is anticipated.

Many have claimed that those on the lower end of the social hierarchy, the so-called lower classes, can have but little feeling of commitment to the existing social system because they cannot reasonably expect to achieve any significant upward mobility within their time horizon, which for most people is their own lifetime plus perhaps that of their children. The only way in which upward mobility can really be affected is by luck, fate, or by overthrowing the existing social structure. However, near subsistence living dictates conservatism and low-level skills, which means that at least that part of the lower class living at near subsistence level rarely provides the necessary leadership and will to innovate socially or politically. Rather, it is very likely to be exceedingly conservative, poverty being rationalized by a religious dogma that places little value on material, mortal achievement — a situation that has prevailed in Turkey until very recently. In such a situation, rapid secularization can cause massive unrest.

Certain members of the upper class may likewise see the existing social structure as dysfunctional in that they can no longer achieve (or innovate) within it. They have hit the limitations imposed by the traditional relationships within the system. By no longer achieving within the system, the upper class generates pressure to develop a new system that will permit additional achievement. This pressure may become compelling, as indeed it did in Turkey under the leadership of Mustafa Kemal Atatürk. There is a natural alliance, then, between certain members of the upper class and of the upper lower class, the latter being defined in terms of a subsistence-*plus* level of living but consisting of those still locked in the vicious circle of low skill–low productivity–low income–absence of educational opportunity. What has been added are expectations.

This model also suggests an explanation for another pattern of behavior. Reference is made to those situations in which age is a predominant factor in determining one's status and in which university student population tends to consist very largely of the sons of the upper middle class. Such youth are likely to anticipate achievement, in that they anticipate movement into the upper class. But their age frustrates immediate movement into such status. We could almost predict a pattern of behavior which would encompass youthful radicalism at the university age, because the social system fails to satisfy strongly felt needs, and growing conservatism as the individual grows in age and, hence, in social status. In Turkey, university student population has probably been more representative of the upper class, or the older, more stable part of the middle class, and, hence, less radical in its views. We would suspect, however, that this situation is beginning to change — particularly in the newer universities.

Obviously, this model does not concur completely with reality. The reason is that it needs to be set into motion. For example, if movement between the upper middle class and the upper class is too restrained institutionally to constitute a reasonable expectation by members of the upper middle class, a middle-class-led revolt can be anticipated, not conservatism and stability. This situation prevailed in the later years of Sultan Abdul Hamid's reign, but is not so true today. If there is a free and easy international movement of persons, so that upper-class nationals can escape the restraints imposed on achievement and innovation within their own society and achieve within a larger, external society, then their own existing social structure may be functional for them. It provides the springboard. An upper-class and an upper-lower-class alliance in revolt, as suggested above, may thus be ruled out. The upper class is not at home to lead it. In a sense, then, foreign exchange and emigration controls may stimulate internal change by keeping a rebellious elite at home.

What happens if the whole system is speeded up, as has happened in the Turkish case? A dichotomy appears. That is, a new and old middle class, a new and old upper class, and a new and old lower class will all exist at the same time.

The faster the process, the larger the "new" group will be at all levels. Note that the *new* lower class consists of middle-class fallouts; the new upper class, of middle-class climbers. But the new middle class consists of both *lower-class climbers* and *upper-class fallouts*. We would suggest that the groups perceiving the present social structure as least satisfying are the upper-class fallouts (i.e., a part of the new middle class) and the middle-class fallouts (i.e., the new lower class). There is a time dimension to these upper- and middle-class fallouts in that the fall may be represented by a slow or rapid downgrading. If too rapid, it may lead to complete alienation from society. If too slow, it may generate no positive response. In the Turkish case, the movement seems to have been very close to optimal from the point of view of generating a positive response.

Who constitutes Turkey's *new* middle class (i.e., the upper-class fallouts and the lower-class climbers) and the *old* middle class? It is important to make these distinctions if there is any concern with maximum return on educational investment, for it is likely to be the upper-class fallouts who are at once the most ambitious and most rebellious unless avenues are opened whereby they can hope to recapture their lost positions without major overhaul of the social system. The reopened avenues can be a promise of reward for the achievement of useful, high-level skills — that is, educational opportunity.

The ingredients of the *old* middle class would surely include many of the petty bourgeois (the *esnaf* or trade guild members), the ordinary bureaucrat, the undistinguished military officer, and the run-of-the-mill professional man. In all cases, their fathers were of similar origin. These groups survived and prospered under the Kemalist-Inönü eras and are now in their third republican generation. As they rise out of the middle class, they tend to produce a status quo, an almost traditionalist, elite. For them, the social structure of republican Turkey has been adequately satisfying. In general, they and their fathers and grandfathers carried on traditional skills needed and valued in both Ottoman and republican Turkey. Hence, the businessman is not among this group.

As already noted, the *new* middle class consists of upper-class fallouts and lower-class climbers. Among the latter are the same groups as listed for the *old* middle class, but whose fathers were of lower-class origin — most frequently, small landowning farmers or low-level craftsmen. In addition is the businessman of lower-class origin, whose skill was not valued by Ottoman Moslem society. This part of the middle class, sensing the republican social system to be satisfying, tends to produce a conservative elite which avidly supports the Kemalist reforms but which resists further change. Much of the younger military leadership seems to be of this stripe.

Perhaps the key middle-class element is the upper-class fallout. Among the fallouts are:

1. Religious leaders and their sons and grandsons, who under the pressure of secularization have lost status and seek for respected new identities.

2. Village landlords and their near descendants, who lose status as wealth is less and less closely identified with land ownership (witness the fact that the concept of the *ağa* — a traditional rural term of respect for the landed wealthy — is passing; the very term brings smiles to the faces of many contemporary Turks).

3. Urban dwelling members of the rural elite (e.g., large landowners) who are denied elite status in the urban society with which they now identify.

4. Sons and grandsons of former high Ottoman officials who frequently held office on the basis of ascriptive norms (e.g., kinship) rather than achievement.

5. The political associates of Mustafa Kemal and of Ismet Inönü, or their sons, who have been displaced by the emergence of a *local* political elite (i.e., by the Democratic-Justice Party elites), many of whom are now major real estate owners or businessmen in Istanbul and Ankara.

6. The military, as the political regime becomes slowly re-civilianized and the relative wealth of the military falls.

7. The former political associates of Prime Minister Adnan Menderes who were ousted from power and stripped of much of their wealth and income-generating power.

Here we have a number of new middle-class categories, members of which are denied *expected* status in contemporary Turkey. One might anticipate substantial innovational behavior on their part, even to the point of revolt in favor of a more paternalistic-elitist regime. On the other hand, a large part of the elite — the upper class — is new in that it consists of upper-class climbers. The elements moved into the upper class as a result of the Kemalist revolution, the ousting of the Greek and Armenian minorities, the economic impact of World War II, the 1950 election, the 1960 coup, and fairly rapid and persistent inflation. These people tend to see the existing, relatively liberal, non-directed social structure as functional. Hence, they have a tendency toward conservatism.

Given this possible conflict between important elements in the upper and middle classes, as well as between military and civilian, it becomes of even greater importance to keep pressures from building up beyond the critical points which the system can tolerate without being blown apart. If those exerting the greatest pressure on the system — that is, those with the highest need achievement — can somehow be channeled into high-level manpower development programs, Turkey has much to gain in terms of both efficiency of educational investment and continuity of law and order.

Having thus plotted the background against which events and programs in contemporary Turkey should be silhouetted, we proceed to the specific changes occurring in the society relevant to manpower development. One can then derive some rationale for the estimates of high-level manpower demand and supply and of the processes of human capital formation and of allocation. The point of departure is necessarily demographic.

II

DIRECTIONS OF SOCIAL CHANGE

POPULATION

The increase in Turkey's manpower has begun to alarm her political and economic elite, who see in a rising rate of increase a threat to economic growth. The authors of the *First Five-Year Development Plan, 1963–1967* urged a new population policy designed to restrain population growth. Previously, official policy had been designed to accomplish the contrary.[1]

A 1930 law making the Ministry of Public Health responsible for increasing the birthrate also forbade the import and sale of contraceptive devices. The Turkish penal code of 1926 had already made abortion a crime. A 1936 amendment of the code outlawed sterilization and the dissemination of information concerning contraception. Modern planners urged the repeal of these restraints, and a law authorizing the distribution of birth control information and devices became effective on July 10, 1965. An intensive family planning effort is anticipated, and the Turkish government has requested the United States for several hundred jeeps to carry out a rural program toward this end.[2]

The source of alarm on the subject of population growth stems from the set of figures shown in Table 2. It should be noted that the tally in the last line of this table was not available to the writers of the 1963–1967 plan and is based on a very provisional report of the October 24, 1965, census.

TABLE 2. ANNUAL RATE OF POPULATION INCREASE IN TURKEY, 1927–1960

YEAR	PER CENT
1927–1935	1.5830
1936–1940	1.7395
1941–1945	1.9650
1946–1950	2.1970
1951–1955	2.7450
1956–1960	2.9500
(1960–1965)	(2.4300)

Source: *Monthly Bulletin of Statistics,* no. 61 (Ankara: Central Statistical Office, March 1959), pp. 154–55; 1960–65 figure: preliminary report of 1965 census, *Cumhuriyet,* October 30, 1965.

Basis: Censuses of 1927, 1935, 1940, 1945, 1950, 1955, 1960. Annual rate of increase from one census year to the next is assumed to be constant. Annual rates are calculated by formula $A = a(t+r)^n$, where A is population in terminal census; a that in the initial census; r is annual rate of increase; t is number of years between A and a. The 1956–60 rate is calculated from the 1960 census total (27,830,000). If a trend curve is fitted to the annual rates from 1935 forward and extended back to 1927, it will be noticed that the annual rate drops below the 1936–40 rate. Yet, if the published 1927 census were used, the rate for the 1927–35 period would be .021325 per year. Therefore, the rate for this early period has been adjusted by adding 607,730 to the official 1927 census total, which figure represents under counting. Adjustment has also been made for the annexation of the Hatay province in 1939 and for the politically-stimulated influx of refugees from Bulgaria in 1950–51. The 1965 census count was 31,-391,207.

It would appear that there has been a surprising slowing down in the Turkish rate of population growth since 1960, explained in part by some analysts by the absence of some 150,000 Turkish workers employed in western Europe. It would also appear from Table 3 that the percentage of people in Turkey not wanting more children is somewhat lower than in a number of other less developed countries. The changing age composition of the population should likewise be noted, particularly the drop in the 0–9 years category and increase in the 20–45 years category. Otherwise the age pyramid has shown remarkable constancy (see Table 4 and Chart II).

The average life expectancy at birth, according to one estimate, was 57.6 years in 1962,[3] which one suspects was high. Another estimate places life expectancy at 33 years.[4] (Presumably both estimates represent life expectancy at birth.) Projecting present fertility rates into the future, one derives a maximum growth rate of 3.44 per cent by 1980.

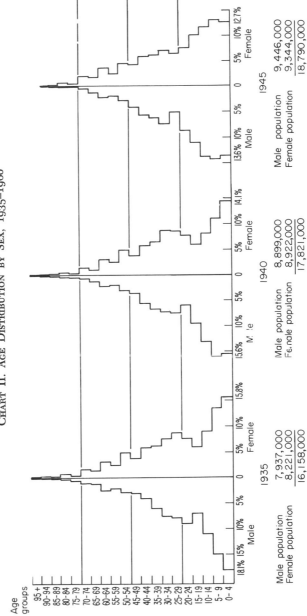

CHART II. AGE DISTRIBUTION BY SEX, 1935–1960

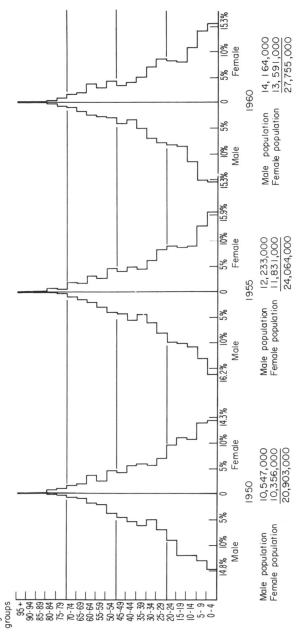

Age
groups

95 +
90-94
85-89
80-84
75-79
70-74
65-69
60-64
55-59
50-54
45-49
40-44
35-39
30-34
25-29
20-24
15-19
10-14
5- 9
0- 4

1950

Male population   10,547,000
Female population   10,356,000
                       20,903,000

Male   14.8% 10% 5% 0 5% 10% 14.3% Female

1955

Male population   12,233,000
Female population   11,831,000
                       24,064,000

Male   16.2% 10% 5% 0 5% 10% 15.9% Female

1960

Male population   14,164,000
Female population   13,591,000
                       27,755,000

Male   15.3% 10% 5% 0 5% 10% 15.3% Female

Source: 1935–1950: *Nüfus Sayîmlarï* (Ankara: Central Statistical Office, 1953), Statistical Résumé no. 8, p. 5.

1955: *İstatistik Yıllığı*, 1959 (Ankara: Central Statistical Office, 1961), pp. 72–77.

1960: *İstatistik Yıllığı*, 1960–62 (Ankara: Central Statistical Office, 1964), pp. 73–75.

TABLE 3. PERCENTAGES OF PERSONS REPORTING THEY DO NOT
WANT MORE CHILDREN

	DATE	AMONG THOSE HAVING		
		3 LIVING CHILDREN	4 LIVING CHILDREN	5 OR MORE LIVING CHILDREN
Puerto Rico	1953	—	87	93
Jamaica	1957	68	80	84
Turkey	1963	23	44	66
East Pakistan	1963	50	56	63
West Pakistan	1960	38	67	73
India	1958	42	75	85
Ceylon	1962	57	69	88
Taiwan	1962–63	54	76	88
Thailand	1964	71	86	88
Japan	1961	95	98	96
Indonesia	1961	23	37	41
Philippines	1963	56	68	85

Source: W. Parker Mauldin, "Fertility Studies: Knowledge, Attitude, and
Practice," Studies in Family Planning, no. 7, 1965, p. 7.

TABLE 4. POPULATION BY AGE GROUPS
(percentages)

AGE	0–9	10–19	20–29	30–39	40–49 (45–46)	50–59	60–69 (60–61)	70+	UNKNOWN
1927	48.0			36.3 (39.0)		10.2		5.3	.2
1935	31.4	16.4	16.9	13.8	8.3	6.0	4.2	2.6	.4
	47.8			30.7					
1940	29.8	20.8	13.6	14.0	9.3	5.9	4.1	2.4	.1
1945	26.9	23.1	13.8	13.9	10.0	5.9	4.1	2.2	.1
1950	26.8	22.5	16.4	11.5	10.0	6.5	3.9	2.0	.2
1955	29.4	19.5	17.8	10.5	9.5	6.9	3.9	2.2	.2
1960	29.6	19.8	16.6	12.4	7.7	6.5	4.4	2.8	.2
	49.4			44.7	(45–46) 8.5		(60–61) 7.2		

Sources: 1927 figures from Nüfus Sayïmlarï (Ankara: Central Statistical
Office, 1953), p. 5.

1935–50: Nüfus Sayïmlarï (Ankara: Central Statistical Office, 1953), Statistical Résumé, no. 8, p. 5.

1955: İstatistik Yïlliği, 1959 (Ankara: Central Statistical Office, 1961), pp.
72–77.

1960: İstatistik Yïlliği, 1960–62 (Ankara: Central Statistical Office, 1964),
pp. 73–75.

However, economic pressure, urbanization, and official encouragement may combine to push the fertility rate down, which would mean that the net rate of growth will level off shortly. The 1965 census indicates that this may have already occurred. Turkey's planners have summarized their estimates as shown in Tables 5 and 6.

The following observations should be made:

1. The percentage of aged (65+) does not change significantly for the three projections in Tables 5 and 6.

2. For the population under 15 years of age, the fertility rate can make a difference of 7.4 per cent by 1985, the high rate producing the highest percentages of children.

3. For the active population, the fertility rate may alter the 1985 estimate by 6.9 per cent, the high rate producing the lowest percentage of active population.

4. The absolute number of active people will not differ significantly with the three fertility rates, the spread being only 571,000 out of 51 million or more.

5. But the absolute difference in the numbers of children is quite large, being 7,278,000.

It should be noted that the lower fertility rates would facilitate the entry of more women into the labor force, and, by reducing the proportion of children, (1) should increase the savings rate, (2) reduce investment required in general education, and (3) reduce consumption per worker. For these several reasons, Turkey's planners have pushed for a new population policy which hopefully would tend to reduce the fertility rate.

POPULATION MOVEMENTS

Coincident with the rising growth rate of Turkey's population and its changing age composition has been a rush to the cities. Particularly since 1950, the rural-urban movement has been gathering momentum (see Chart III). The annual

TABLE 5. POPULATION PROJECTIONS ASSUMING VARYING RATES
OF INCREASE, 1960–1985
(in thousands)

POPULATION	1960	1965	1970	1975	1980	1985
High fertility........	27,830	31,996	36,697	42,558	49,947	59,162
Medium fertility.....	27,830	31,936	36,401	41,579	47,744	55,016
Low fertility.........	27,830	31,936	36,106	40,635	45,701	51,313
Life expectancy at birth (in years)....	57.6	60.4	63.2	65.8	68.2	
ANNUAL RATE OF INCREASE (per 1000)						
High fertility........	27.9	28.2	30.0	32.5	34.4	
Medium fertility.....	27.9	26.6	27.0	28.0	28.7	
Low fertility.........	27.9	24.9	23.9	23.8	23.4	

Source: *First Five-Year Development Plan, 1963–1967*. Ankara: Union of Chambers of Commerce, Industry and Commodity Exchanges of Turkey, 1963, p. 66.

TABLE 6. PROJECTED AGE COMPOSITION OF POPULATION, 1960–1985
(According to the assumptions of high, medium, and low fertility)
(in thousands)

	1960	1965	1970	1975	1980	1985
0—14						
High	11,910	13,757	15,506	17,896	21,401	26,035
Medium	11,910	13,757	15,210	16,917	19,198	22,173
Low	11,910	13,757	14,915	15,973	17,155	18,757
15—64						
High	14,919	16,937	19,663	22,844	26,422	30,882
Medium	14,919	16,937	19,663	22,844	26,422	30,596
Low	14,919	16,937	19,663	22,844	26,422	30,311
65+						
High	1,001	1,242	1,528	1,818	2,124	2,245
Medium	1,001	1,242	1,528	1,818	2,124	2,245
Low	1,001	1,242	1,528	1,818	2,124	2,245
PERCENTAGE DISTRIBUTION						
0—14						
High	42.8	43.1	42.3	42.1	42.9	44.0
Medium	42.8	43.1	41.8	40.7	40.2	40.3
Low	42.8	43.1	41.3	39.3	37.5	36.6
15—64						
High	53.6	53.0	53.5	53.6	52.9	52.2
Medium	53.6	53.0	54.0	54.9	55.3	55.6
Low	53.6	53.0	54.5	56.2	57.8	59.1
65+						
High	3.6	3.9	4.2	4.3	4.3	3.8
Medium	3.6	3.9	4.2	4.4	4.5	4.1
Low	3.6	3.9	4.2	4.5	4.6	4.4

Source: *Five-Year Plan*, p. 67.

CHART III. PERCENTAGE OF POPULATION IN CITIES, 1927–1960

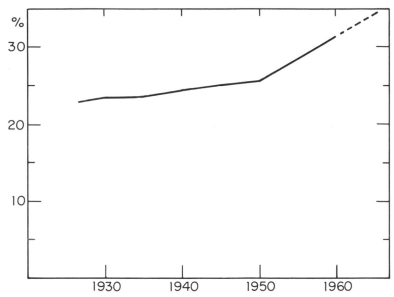

Source: Same as for Table 2.
Basis: 1927 census has been adjusted as described in the note under Table 2.

flow may now equal 3 per cent of the rural population, which means that the latter has reached a plateau.[5] Pressures generating this internal migration have been: (1) a land squeeze (a function of farm mechanization, population explosion, eruption of economic incentive); (2) inter-generation frictions (a function of exposure to modern military training and urban life by members of the younger generation, plus the traditionalism of village elders); (3) vastly improved transportation and communication; and (4) access to education and public health institutions. Not only has this been an urban movement generally, but the highly traditional nature of small-town society has diverted this flow around the provincial market towns and directly into the larger cities. Note the growth of the largest urban centers as shown in

TABLE 7. POPULATION OF MAJOR CITIES

CITY	1927	1940	1950	1960	1965
Istanbul	690,857	793,949	983,041	1,466,535	1,750,642
Ankara	74,553	157,242	288,536	650,067	902,216
Izmir	153,924	183,762	227,578	360,829	417,411
Adana	72,577	88,119	117,642	231,548	219,000
Bursa	61,690	77,598	103,812	153,866	213,000
Eskişehir	32,341	60,742	89,870	153,096	174,000
Gaziantep	39,998	57,132	71,887	124,097	na
Konya	47,496	56,465	64,434	119,841	na
Kayseri	39,134	52,467	65,488	102,596	na
TOTAL	1,213,570	1,527,476	2,021,297	3,362,475	

Sources: 1927–50, 22 *Ekim 1950 Umumi Nüfus Sayĭmĭ* (Ankara, İstatistik Umum Müdürlüğü, no. 359), p. 32; 1960, 23 *Ekim 1960 Genel Nüfus Sayĭmĭ* (Ankara: Devlet İstatistik Enstitüsü, 1963), p. xli.

Table 7. The need for new housing, new urban service, new skills, and new employment on the part of these new urban dwellers has sorely taxed the resources of government. Yet, political factors require that at least minimum standards be maintained.

In addition to this permanent resettlement, there is a very large transient labor force, of both a seasonal and an exploratory nature. Among the first to leave a village are the younger sons of the economically oppressed families who need sources of income alternative to agriculture. Undoubtedly, a major part of this transient group eventually joins the permanent urban group. But still, this means that at any one time there is, in the big cities, a large floating male population composed principally of younger men, not infrequently of school age.

There is reason to believe that the large urban centers — principally Ankara and Istanbul — are magnets for the more dynamic elements of the population elsewhere, namely the ambitious, the wealthy, the intellectual, the skilled, the politician, the creative, the frustrated, even the criminal. The growth element is thus being siphoned off the rest of the country, and the disparity between these centers and the balance of the country widens. There is no evidence that a significant number of urbanized villagers are returning to the countryside other than for an occasional visit.

Emigration and immigration have not been significant and probably will not be in the foreseeable future, except for the skilled or semi-skilled worker now seeking employment in western Europe, of which more will be said later.

A related subject is the dispersion of the population. From 1955 to 1960, the number of villages actually grew from 34,787 to 35,444, and there was some discernible shift in village size upwards, the number of villages in the 0–300 person category dropping and the number claiming more than 300 persons, increasing.[6] This dispersion of population is an important restraint upon the organization of an efficient general education program, for many of the communities are too small and isolated to participate in centralized school units.

SOCIAL RESTRAINTS

Relevant to any discussion of manpower development are the social restraints or rigidities imbedded in the social structure. According to the 1960 census, some 7.3 per cent of the population claimed Kurdish as their mother tongue. It is quite possible that at least twice that number, in fact, identify themselves as Kurds, and would be so identified by the majority Turkish ethnic group. Generally speaking, Kurds are not accepted in top military or administrative posts, but are nonetheless regarded more highly than other ethnic groups — Arabs, Greeks, Jews, Armenians — none of which are present in large numbers.

The Alevis or Shiites constitute the largest religious minority, which is distinct from the Moslem majority of Sunni persuasion. This minority probably numbers close to 25 per cent of the population.[7] At the village level, Shiite and Sunni rarely intermarry and frequently do not consider each other as coreligionists. With the recent release of controls over religious activity, plus improved communications, the Alevi minority has apparently felt vulnerable in their villages, and a disproportionately large number of them seem to be joining the move into the big cities. Typically, the Alevis are less traditionalist than the Sunnis at the rural level, perhaps a result of being compelled to live by their wits, including deceit, in a hostile social climate. One suspects that both Kurd and Alevi groups may be the source of considerable creativity if Everett E. Hagen's "denial of expected status" thesis is at all valid.[8] Hence, it becomes important to design manpower development programs that are both attractive and open to these groups — a subject not often discussed in the more popular journals in Turkey.

The other religious minority groups — the Jews and Christians — are much too small to be significant. They usually live in enclaves in Istanbul or Izmir, educating their children in private schools, and, although dominating much of the commercial life of these two cities, are quite alienated from the predominately Turkish-Moslem society surrounding them. These groups cannot be expected to constitute an important part of the *effective,* creative element within Turkish society in the near future.

A heavy hand of traditionalism rests on the status of the female population. Even today, of 313 million children in the primary schools, 64 per cent are boys. Of the 355,000 in middle school (grades 6, 7, 8), 76 per cent are boys. In 1960, 75 per cent of the women were illiterate, as compared to 46.3 per cent of the men.[9] There is some evidence that in recent years, given the politically-motivated relaxation of police pressure, the proportion of girls in the schools has not risen (see Table 8). Clearly, the percentage of girls in village schools did not increase between 1945 and 1958, a fact which

TABLE 8. STUDENT REGISTRATION IN TURKEY'S PRIMARY SCHOOLS BY SEX

	1936–37		1945–50		1958–59		1962–63	
	Boys	Girls	Boys	Girls	Boys	Girls	Boys	Girls
Village primary	69%	31%	65%	35%	65%	35%	64%	36%
Urban primary	66	34	59	41	58	42	57	43
Total primary	67	33	63	37	62	38	61	39

Source: İstatistik Yıllığı, 1952, p. 159; İstatistik Yıllığı, 1960–62, p. 142.

was confirmed by personal observation in Anatolian villages after 1950. Since 1960, this trend may have reversed slightly.

In that the inferior status of the female is probably a function of the near subsistence economy and isolation,[10] an eventual upgrading of women's position can be anticipated. The apparent breakdown of the arranged marriage system would seem to indicate that a basic change is in fact occurring. Still, many restraints operate against full participation by women in the society and make unlikely their easy entry into many occupations which would otherwise be suitable for women. Nursing is an example. Also, it would be unthinkable for a woman to be a transient worker unless she were accompanied by her husband. If married, the chances are that she would move to the city with her husband only if he were settling there permanently. Otherwise, she would be left behind in the village. Of course, prolonged absence of the male can force a breakdown in the traditionally imposed occupational specialization by sex in the village, thereby increasing the responsibility of the woman and, hence, her status.

Of all relationships in traditional Turkish society, those of kinship are by all odds the most important, so important that the student-teacher, employee-employer, or citizen-government relationship take on the aspects of the child-parent relationship. Turkish industry, school, government, religion, and the military operate on the basis of a highly developed paternalism involving reciprocal obligations of a strictly personal nature. Loyalties tend to run to persons, not to institutions or to abstract values. This fact limits the motivations to which appeals can be made in generating support for a program of manpower development, a fact the Turkish military has long recognized.

As already indicated, the regional unevenness of the country is being accentuated by the drawing off of the more talented, ambitious, and creative segment of the population into one or two large urban centers in the western part of the country. Hence, this trend constitutes a consideration in the formulation of optimum policies for manpower development. How can these growth elements be held back in their native regions so as to provide catalysts and models for other less dynamic elements? The urban-rural disparity is so great as to constitute a pressing problem in itself. The danger is that the society may be pulled apart into a relatively modern urban elite on one hand and a highly traditional rural mass on the other. The two can easily become more and more alienated one from the other, and finally any program sponsored by the elite may become intolerable to the masses or simply ineffective as control is lost. In the meantime, communication could virtually cease between the two sectors. Fortunately in Turkey there is no clear ethnic or religious distinction that coincides with rural-urban division, so that this process may be slowed somewhat and perhaps could be reversed by deliberate programming. The rural-urban distinction is apparent in the relatively greater flow of students through the urban primary schools, as shown in Table 9. It will be noted that the disparity between rural and urban population seems to be widening, perhaps because of a tendency for those families interested in education for their children to join the urban-bound migration.

Political restraints have surfaced several times in this discussion. The extent to which manpower development can be forced by a modernizing urban elite is at least related to: (1)

TABLE 9. URBAN-RURAL DISTRIBUTION OF ELEMENTARY EDUCATION, 1955, 1960

	1955	1960
Urban population	6,927,343	8,881,542
Urban elementary school population	666,247	978,358
Percentage in elementary schools	9.6%	11.0%
Rural population	17,137,420	18,873,278
Rural elementary school population	1,296,749	1,585,837
Percentage in elementary schools	7.5%	7.9%

Source: Andreas M. Kazamias, "Education and the Quest for Modernity in Turkey: Origins and Growth" (Madison: University of Wisconsin, 1965, typed ms.), Table V, p. 321. Figures include private elementary schools. Urban population relates to places with a population of 10,000 or more.

the degree of effective communication between the two groups — urban elite and rural mass; (2) the degree of national commitment by the elite; (3) the degree of centralized authority in its hands; and (4) perhaps the absence of a mass partisan political organization. A too rapid liberalization of political institutions or a too direct participation in political organization could conceivably force a return to traditional concepts, which might well slow up the shift from traditionalism to modernism and, hence, of development generally. There is also the inherent conflict between the consumption function of the elite and that of the mass in a near subsistence economy newly moved by economic incentive. This subject was touched upon in the introductory paragraphs.

MANPOWER DEVELOPMENT

School Attendance. The 1960 census revealed that 39.5 per cent of the population was literate, a decline of 1.4 per cent from 1955. The decline showed up for both men (53.6 per cent in 1960, 55.8 per cent in 1955) and women (24.8 per cent and 25.5 per cent).[11] This backsliding was undoubtedly produced by the reduction of police pressure behind the compulsory education law following the advent of a multiparty system in 1950 as well as the unequal growth of school facilities and the number of school-age children. The decline could not be explained by the increase in number of pre-school children, for percentages given above excluded all children below the age of six. It will be noted from the figures in Table 10 that although there was a substantial in-

TABLE 10. SCHOOL ATTENDANCE IN ABSOLUTE NUMBERS
AND AS PERCENTAGES OF SCHOOL-AGE CHILDREN, 1955, 1961

AGES	1955		1961	
6–11 (Primary, grades 1–5)	1,983,668	(58%)	3,160,000	(70%)
12–14 (Middle, grades 6–8)	252,206	(18)	401,400	(23)
15–17 (Lycée, grades 9–12)	57,990	(4)	132,500	(9)
18–21 (Higher)	36,998	(2)	61,000	(4)
7–22 (All education)	2,330,862	(29%)	3,754,900	(39%)

Source: For 1955, İstatistik, 1960–62, pp. 73, for 1961, Five-Year Plan, p. 422.

Turkish and U.S. enrollment ratios given in Targets for Education in Europe in 1970 (Paris: OECD Policy Conference on Economic Growth and Investment in Education, 1962), p. 110:

For age groups:	5–14	15–19	20–24	5–24
In Turkey, 1959/60	44.0%	3.3%	1.1%	25.1%
In the U.S., 1959/60	89.0%	66.2%	12.0%	69.9%

Note: Educational categories include technical and vocational schools of the designated levels. Percentage figures are only approximate, because schools of various levels would draw on a larger range of age groups. The percentages for primary school are unrealistically high, but would not be if the 12- and 13-year age groups were added in, likewise part of the 5-year age group. The 6-year age group has been included.

crease in the percentages of children of the primary and middle school categories that were reported to be attending school, one should also mark the significant break between the primary and middle school systems.

Student Flow. The distribution of students in the public school system during the 1962–63 school year is shown in Chart IV. In his analysis of Turkish education for the Research and Management Bureau of the Turkish Ministry of Education, Jefferson N. Eastmond found that during the 1950–60 decade the percentage of the population with five years of schooling had increased from 11.5 per cent to 15.2 per cent, and that the per cent with more education had

CHART IV. DISTRIBUTION OF TURKISH YOUTH POPULATION ENROLLED
IN PUBLIC SCHOOLS IN SCHOOL YEAR, 1962–1963

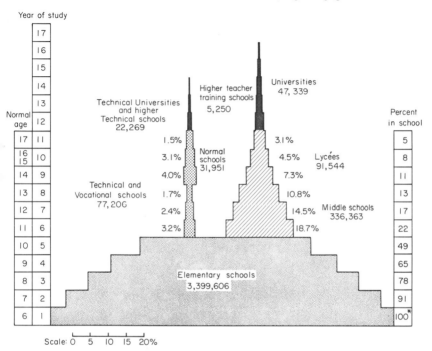

Scale: 0   5   10   15   20%

Source: "Report on Developments in Education During the 1962–63
School Year" (Turkish Ministry of Education, presented to XXVI Educational Conference in Geneva, July 1963), p. 14.
     * Note: Because the "Per Cent in School" is calculated on the basis of the total
number of children of "Normal Age" for that grade, it may exceed 100% since the
grade contains children of other ages besides the "Normal Age."

remained practically constant — eight years of schooling at
about 2 per cent, eleven years of schooling at less than 1 per
cent, and university graduates at less than one-half of 1 per
cent.[12]

Health. There are few firm statistics relating to the health
of the Turkish population. One important observation is the
regional unevenness of the services available in the country.
For example, in the province of Istanbul there were 635 per-

sons per medical doctor in 1959. At the same time, in 18 provinces scattered through the central and eastern part of the country, there were 15,342 persons per doctor. As of mid-1966, there were 53,000 medical doctors in the provinces of Istanbul, Ankara, and Izmir; 4,000 served the other 64 provinces. Another disparity in available health facilities is bared by the fact that in 1959 there were 74.7 hospital beds per 10,000 inhabitants in Istanbul, but only 3 to 10 hospital beds per 10,000 in such places as Hakkâri and Adana.

Of the total population of 24 million in 1955, it was officially reported that 23.7 million were fundamentally healthy, in the sense of not being blind, crippled, or otherwise permanently incapacitated. All measures of medical treatment such as hospital admittances, inoculations, various forms of treatment, as well as the number of medical personnel available are reported to be increasing at a rate more rapid than the general population. This gradual improvement of medical facilities is largely a result of direct government involvement, particularly in the small provincial towns of the eastern provinces where private practitioners have been very reluctant to reside.[13] Indeed, one of the more compelling arguments in favor of government participation in providing medical services to the population is this reluctance of private practitioners to leave the environs of Istanbul, Ankara, and two or three other of the larger cities. Frequently, only doctors in government service can be induced to serve in the more isolated communities.

Although cause-of-death statistics are limited to the municipal districts, these would indicate that heart disease and pneumonia are by all odds the major killers. For some fifteen or twenty years now the government has maintained preventive campaigns against malaria, trachoma, and tuberculosis, all of which used to be important fatal and debilitating diseases. The incidence of these diseases has been cut down significantly. This effort has possibly contributed, to a statistically significant degree, to the dramatic reduction in the death rate and hence, to the population explosion. It is still estimated that in many rural areas something in the neighborhood of one or two of every five children born alive die within the first year of life. One suspects that many of these births are never recorded. Hence, these doomed infants are not included in any of the statistical reports published by the Turkish government.

For some years, the Ministry of Health and Social Welfare has been trying to improve facilities available to expectant mothers in both urban and rural areas, including an expanding program for training midwives. A recent study produced an estimate that the infant mortality rate had dropped from 18 per cent in 1935–1940 to 13 per cent in 1950–1955. Death rates for the older groups had likewise declined. The result was that life expectancy was estimated to have increased from about 44.9 years to 52.7 over the 1935–1955 period.[14] However, there is much doubt about the validity of such estimates, as has already been noted.

There is no evidence of serious malnutrition in the country, although some authorities have speculated that the intake of animal protein may be sufficiently low as to limit the energy output of a significant part of the population. There is, however, no real evidence establishing this to be the case.

The directions of social change in Turkey are thus plotted: a high rate of population growth — though possibly now falling; a large-scale, selective, movement of countryfolk into the cities; a magnetic pull of the two large urban centers — Istanbul and Ankara; a dramatic increase in the movement of people throughout the country; the continued residence of a large but diminishing part of the population in village communities; a significant division by ethnic identity, religion, sex, and residence; the continuing role of kinship and personal loyalties. There would appear to have been a recent slowing down of educational development compared to the growth of the population, resulting in a drop-off in the literacy rate and an unchanging proportion of rural girls in school. Nor is there any indication that the break between primary and secondary school is being bridged. Finally, steady improvement in the health and longevity of the population is reported.

In short, the dynamics of the present social-political structure leads one to the conclusion that the climate is right for a major manpower development effort and that the return on a massive investment in people would be high. But investment requires resources.

III

DIRECTIONS OF
ECONOMIC CHANGE

INCOME LEVELS

As a rough aggregate measure of economic change, growth in per capita national income since World War II may be cited. In 1948, it stood at TL 440, reached a high at TL 604 (in constant 1948 prices) in 1959, and has remained at roughly the same level since then (e.g., 528 in 1965).[1] No firm estimate of income distribution is available, but it is significant that in 1960 Turkish planners estimated that roughly 9.3 per cent of the rural population owned 50 per cent of the farm land and 30.6 per cent owned but 4.3 per cent of the land. Also, there is no evidence that yields of basic grain crops have increased significantly over recent years.[2] With the growth of modern industry and modern agriculture, given the inequities in the tax structure, income distribution has very likely grown more uneven during the post World War II decades. One countervailing force has been inflation, with those in the near subsistence, agricultural barter economy being the least affected. The wholesale price index (1948 = 100) moved from about 22 in 1938, to 100 in 1948, to 202 in 1950, to 227 in 1952, to 310 in 1965. In general, Turkey is moving toward the upper range of partially-developed countries, "Level II," in the Harbison-Myers typology.[3]

BALANCE OF TRADE

From 1938 to the present, Turkey's terms of trade have gradually but steadily worsened. The index for export prices stood at 23 in 1938 and for import, at 24 (1948 = 100) and in 1963, at 248 and 339, respectively.[4] Trade deficits were recorded every year from 1947 onward for a total 1947–1965 deficit of something like $2.3 billion. Meanwhile, Turkey's foreign debt rose to something like $2.4 billion by the end of 1965, with an annual debt service in 1965 of $214 million.[5] The continuing viability of the Turkish economy rests primarily on intergovernmental grants and loans, principally from the United States in the 1948–1955 period, increasingly from European and international financial sources thereafter. Private capital movements contributed only a small amount.[6] Comparative figures for 1965 are shown (at current prices) in Table 11.

TABLE 11. SOME SIGNIFICANT MEASURES, 1965
(in millions)

Gross national product (current prices)	TL 72,317
Exports	4,129
Imports	5,193
Deficit on balance of payments, current accounts	684
Foreign aid	4,500
Foreign debt (estimated)	21,900
Internal debt (estimated)	16,600
Public budgets (national), expenditures	14,012

Sources: Debt: *Middle East and African Economist,* March 1966, p. 37; Foreign Aid: U.S., *ibid.,* May 1966, p. 67; OECD, *ibid.,* April 1965, p. 53; GNP, Exports, Imports, B/P deficit: *Review of Economic Conditions,* May–June 1966, pp. 13–15; Public Budgets, *ibid.,* p. 14.

INVESTMENT

Part of the pressure on Turkey's balance of payments was generated by a high level of investment, varying between an estimated 9.6 per cent of GNP in 1950 to 15.9 per cent in

1960 (11.6 in 1964),[7] plus an increasing level of imports and level of consumption as economic incentives became politically compelling. Meanwhile, the percentage of public expenditures (including public investment) rose with but few hesitations from 17.6 per cent in 1950 to 22.4 per cent in 1964. In 1965 public investment stood at 10.5 per cent of GNP and private, at 7.1 per cent (comparable 1960 figures: 6.9 and 7.2 per cent).[8] During the 1927–1964 period, agriculture's estimated contribution to GNP dropped from 67 per cent in 1927 to 32 per cent in 1965.[9] Another key figure is that for military expenditures, which averaged 25 to 30 per cent of the general budget throughout this period, or about 3.8 to 4.9 per cent of GNP. Comparable figures for public education and health were 10 to 12 per cent and 1.5 to 2 per cent, respectively.[10] Total investment in education and public health is shown in Table 12.

Quite apart from the generally low level of investment in education (1.6 to 2.3 per cent of the GNP),[11] the investment

TABLE 12. EXPENDITURES FOR EDUCATION AND PUBLIC HEALTH, 1947–1963

EXPENDITURE ITEMS		1947–50	1953–56	1960–63
For education				
Current expenditures (millions)	TL	647.7	1,346.4	5,596.7
Real expenditures (millions)*		647.7	1,007.1	2,057.6
Students, number		1,697,777	2,198,700	3,866,232
Per student real exp.	TL	381	490	532
Public health				
Current expenditures (millions)		206.9	500.1	1,660.4
Real expenditures (millions)*		206.9	400.1	610.4
Population, number		20,281,000	23,753,000	29,108,000
Per capita real exp.	TL	10.2	16.8	20.9

Sources: Price indices, *Aylik*, August–December 1960, p. 36; August 1964, p. 60.

Education, *İstatistik, 1949*, p. 263; *ibid., 1953*, pp. 497–98; *ibid., 1956*, p. 465; *ibid., 1960–62*, p. 408.

Students, *Five-Year Plan*, p. 424; *İstatistik, 1959*, p. 145; *ibid., 1960–62*, p. 142.

Population, *Five-Year Plan*, p. 12; *İstatistik, 1959*, p. 149; for 1961–63, a 3 per cent growth rate is assumed.

* Deflated by wholesale price index (4-year average, 1947–50 = 100, 1953–56 = 125, 1960–63 = 272.

is spread very unevenly over the country. One analyst made a province-by-province analysis of per capita expenditures for education, per cent of total educational expenditures for buildings and for professional salaries, local revenue for education per pupil, and per cent of total expenditures for education derived from local sources. From this province-by-province tabulation, a composite average ranking of provinces was calculated, the result of which is shown in Chart V. As Jefferson N. Eastmond, the author of the school finance study, observed:

> . . . the provinces in the western part of the nation (1) spend more money per person for schools; (2) are less pressed to expend a sizable portion of their budgets for the construction of buildings; (3) are able to devote a larger percentage of their budgets for professional salaries, and thus attract and retain the best qualified teachers; (4) obtain more revenue per pupil from local sources; and (5) are able to form a larger part of their total school budgets from local sources.[12]

The author went on to point out that the range between the highest and the lowest provinces in respect to each of these measures was strikingly great.[13] That this disparity is perhaps of some significance is suggested by the lower scores made by university applicants. In one study of 2,177 students who took the entrance examination given by the Economics Faculty of the University of Istanbul in 1963, applicants from eastern Anatolia scored, on the average, significantly below applicants from elsewhere, with those from the western part of the country doing the best.[14]

Note that Chart V shows that the twelve lowest ranking provinces are all in the southeast, with only two exceptions. In many of these provinces reside a predominantly Kurdish population, as Table 13 indicates. This table also shows that not only are the Kurdish areas identified by low literacy, but also by a lower-than-average educational investment.

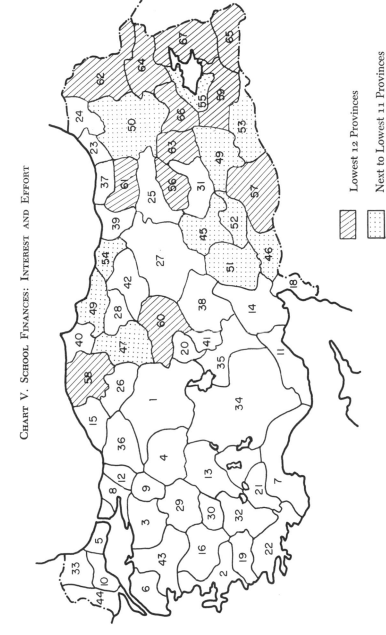

CHART V. SCHOOL FINANCES: INTEREST AND EFFORT

Lowest 12 Provinces

Next to Lowest 11 Provinces

Source: Jefferson N. Eastmond, "School Finance in Turkey" (Ankara: Ministry of Education, 1964), p. 12.

TABLE 13.   EDUCATIONAL STATUS OF THE KURDISH-SPEAKING AREAS, 1960

EASTMOND'S RANKING (SEE CHART V)	PROVINCE	PERCENTAGE OF KURDISH-SPEAKING PEOPLE*	PERCENTAGE OF ILLITERATES*	PERCENTAGE OF SCHOOLLESS VILLAGES*
53	Mardin	91%	86%	71%
59	Siirt	87	84	69
65	Hakkâri	81	88	51
63	Bingöl	68	83	40
49	Diyarbakir	67	80	64
55	Bitlis	66	84	50
57	Urfa	64	84	63
64	Ağrî	61	83	69
66	Muş	53	87	63
67	Van	52	84	69

* Source: M. Şukru Koç, "Barzani ve Doğu Üzerine," Cumhuriyet, 31 July 1966, p. 2.

Safe generalizations that can be made for the post World War II decades are:

1. Per capita income in real terms has moved forward, but slowly.

2. Income distribution has become more uneven.

3. A significant structural shift from the agricultural to non-agricultural sectors has occurred.

4. Inflation has continued but with sporadic halts.

5. Terms of trade have worsened.

6. Uninterrupted balance of payments deficits have been recorded.

7. The role of the government in consumption and investment has expanded.

8. Public expenditures (in real terms) for education per student, and for public health per capita have increased, but unevenly from region to region.

The figures for education and public health would show a higher rate of increase if that portion of relevant military expenditures were included, plus health and education expenditure by the private sector. Other relevant expenditures, likewise impossible to quantify, would be those expenditures on food and housing which improve health, energy level, and longevity — and hence, productivity. Such expenditures are distinct from pure consumption in that they enter into the production function.

On the subject of educational expenditures generally, Jefferson Eastmond found that:

While expenditures for education have increased significantly since 1947, these appear much less than Turkey's high birth rate if the inflation of the Turkish lira is taken into consideration. Moreover, while the percentage of Turkey's gross national product devoted to education has risen from 1.53% in 1948 to 2.2% in 1962, this still represents a very modest effort on behalf of education.[15]

He concluded that "Turkey could triple the percentage of its gross national product that it spends for education and still be spending only a modest percentage in relation to that expended in other nations," the United States expending about 6.2 per cent of its national income on education compared to Turkey's 2.3 per cent. He noted a decrease from 1960 to 1964 in "current" expenditures (i.e., excluding investment in buildings) per elementary school pupil (from 202 lira in 1960 to 198 lira in 1963), which he observed, ". . . is the best single index to reveal a deterioration in the quality of Turkish education."[16]

It would seem apparent that for Turkey to meet the financial requirements implied in its manpower development goals, external assistance will be needed. Perhaps a prototype of one sort is the 7.5 million deutschmark grant from the West German government announced in August 1966 for the organization of Turkey's first technical school to train engineers and skilled labor for the textile industry. The teaching staff is to be supplied by Germany for the first five years.

IV

HIGH-LEVEL MANPOWER DEMAND

ESTIMATES OF DEMAND

The Turkish development plan (1963–67) details present and projected future demands for high-level manpower. Projections are based on "coefficients of labor force production elasticity," calculated from the employment-production series of the past ten years and assume the realization of the production targets defined by the plan. These coefficients were corrected for productivity increases due to expected technological and structural changes induced by the plan (see Tables 17–20). As of 1961, 81 per cent of the active population was employed in agriculture, 9 per cent in industry, 11 per cent in services. Within the industrial sector 7 per cent were employed in mining, 72 per cent in manufacturing and 21 per cent in construction.[1] Within the service sector in 1959, 0.2 per cent of the labor force were scientists and engineers; 0.1 per cent were medical doctors, pharmacists, and veterinarians, 0.2 per cent, secondary and higher teachers.[2]

Of the 1960 labor force total of roughly 13 million, about 10.8 million were in class D occupations (those demanding less than secondary school), slightly over 1.6 million in the class C category (sales, crafts, proprietorial and similar occupations for which secondary education is desirable), 119,000 in class B (occupations requiring technical or semi-professional skills and two or three years of education be-

TABLE 14. OCCUPATIONAL AND EDUCATIONAL QUALIFICATION
OF TURKEY'S ACTIVE POPULATION, 1960

OCCUPATIONAL CATEGORY	ACTUAL No. OF PERSONS 1000's	% OF TOTAL	RELEVANT EDUCATIONAL QUALIFICATION	No. OF PERSONS SATISFYING EDUC. QUAL. 1000's	% OF THOSE NEEDED
A	199	2%	University and higher technical	105	53%
B	119	1	Technical school	112	94
C	1,642	13	Secondary or vocational school	346	21
D	10,800	84	Primary school	2,830	26
Agriculture	9,703	76	Unspecified	na	na
Others	1,097	8	Unspecified	na	na
All classes	12,670	100		(3,393)	

Source: *Turkey* (Paris: OECD Education and Development Country Projects, Mediterranean Regional Project, 1965), p. 45.

yond secondary school), and just over 199,000 in class A (professional and higher-level managerial positions normally requiring higher education).[3] How well the Turkish categories related to the educational requirements for each is reflected in Table 14. Further breakdowns are shown in Tables 15 and 16, which represent the initial values for the projected series shown in Tables 17–19. Turkish planners expect to bring about significant sectoral shifts in manpower utilization as indicated in Tables 17 through 20.

TABLE 15. TURKISH EMPLOYMENT

	1955	1960
Agriculture	9,446,102	9,737,489
Extractive industry	62,645	77,329
Manufacturing industry	726,522	884,669
Construction industry	200,204	290,084
Power industry	16,071	15,484
Commerce, banking, insurance	340,992	403,764
Transport, communications	189,766	246,839
Services	496,281	676,838
Undefined	726,684	660,759
	12,205,267	12,993,255

Source: *İstatistik, 1960–62*, p. 81.

TABLE 16. FUNCTIONAL BREAKDOWN IN SUB-SECTORS OF INDUSTRY
AND IN SERVICES, 1961
(in thousands)

FUNCTIONAL CATEGORIES	MINING	MANUFAC-TURING	CONSTRUC-TION	SERVICES	TOTAL	%
Administrators and entrepreneurs	1.0	8.2	1.3	60.5	71.0	2.6
Professional personnel	0.6	4.2	5.2	61.0	71.0	2.6
Technicians	1.3	6.8	9.1	118.0	136.0	5.0
Lower echelon and sales employees	3.3	20.2	6.8	479.7	510.0	18.5
Foremen	8.2	17.0	7.8	14.0	47.0	1.7
Skilled workers	29.0	317.0	109.0	202.0	657.0	23.8
Unskilled workers	26.6	476.6	120.8	634.0	1,258.0	45.7
TOTAL	70.0	850.0	260.0	1,570.0	2,750.0	100.0

Source: *Five-Year Plan*, p. 420.

TABLE 17. BREAKDOWN OF LABOR FORCE BY SECTOR
(in millions)

SECTORS	1962	1963	1964	1965	1966	1967	1972	1977
Agriculture	9.86	10.00	10.14	10.28	10.42	10.56	10.86	11.16
Industry	1.25	1.34	1.44	1.54	1.65	1.77	2.36	2.99
Services	1.63	1.78	1.94	2.12	2.31	2.52	3.64	5.05
TOTAL	12.74	13.12	13.52	13.94	14.38	14.85	16.86	19.20

Source: *Five-Year Plan*, p. 420.

TABLE 18. PERCENTAGE DISTRIBUTION OF LABOR FORCE BY SECTOR

	1963	1965	1967	1977
Agriculture	77.4	71.1	64.4	58.1
Industry	9.8	11.9	14.0	15.6
Services	12.8	17.0	21.6	26.3

Source: *Five-Year Plan*, p. 420.

TABLE 19. BREAKDOWN OF ACTIVE INDUSTRIAL POPULATION BY SUB-SECTORS
(in thousands)

SUB-SECTOR	1962	1963	1964	1965	1966	1967	1972	1977
Mining	70	74	78	81	85	89	110	131
Manufacturing	880	933	990	1,048	1,110	1,177	1,470	1,756
Construction	330	333	372	411	455	504	780	1,103
TOTAL	1,250	1,340	1,440	1,540	1,650	1,770	2,360	2,990

Source: *Five-Year Plan*, p. 421.

TABLE 20. PAST AND PROJECTED DEMAND FOR LABOR IN INDUSTRY AND SERVICES
(in thousands)

CLASSIFICATION	FUNCTIONAL CATEGORIES	1962	1963	1964	1965	1966	1967	1972	1977
A.	Administrators and entrepreneurs	73.0	77.0	81.0	88.0	97.0	106.0	141.0	194.0
A.	Vocational personnel (total)	73.0	78.5	83.0	91.0	103.0	114.0	190.0	227.0
	Engineers	12.0	13.0	14.0	15.0	16.0	17.0	32.0	56.0
	Health personnel	10.0	10.0	10.0	11.0	11.0	12.0	15.0	24.0
	Teachers (secondary and higher)	22.0	24.5	27.0	20.0	39.0	47.0	85.0	106.0
	Others	29.0	31.0	32.0	35.0	37.0	38.0	58.0	91.0
B.	Tech. personnel (total)	142.0	151.5	165.0	177.0	194.0	213.0	348.0	570.0
	Technicians	20.0	23.0	25.0	27.0	30.0	33.0	74.0	146.0
	Aux. health person.	10.0	10.0	11.0	11.0	15.0	20.0	35.0	65.0
	Teachers (primary)	50.0	54.5	59.0	63.0	67.0	71.0	106.0	154.0
	Others	62.0	64.0	70.0	76.0	82.0	89.0	133.0	205.0
C.	Lower echelon and sales employees	530.0	580.0	635.0	695.0	765.0	840.0	1245.0	1720.0
C.	Foremen	50.0	55.0	60.0	66.0	73.0	81.0	142.0	270.0
C.	Skilled workers	686.0	740.0	790.0	850.0	980.0	1000.0	1540.0	2570.0
D.	Unskilled workers	1326.0	1438.0	1562.0	1693.0	1810.0	1940.0	2384.0	2439.0
	TOTAL	2880.0	3120.0	3376.0	3660.0	3962.0	4294.0	5990.0	8040.0

Source: *Five-Year Plan*, p. 421. OECD classifications added.

UNDEREMPLOYMENT

Although serious underemployment of Turkey's human resources is reported (Turkey's planners estimate that about
one million workers could be removed from agriculture with
no deleterious effect on production), one can anticipate no
improvement.[4] There is every reason to believe that the population will grow (+3 per cent per year) by a rate faster
than employment opportunities can be created. A 3 per cent
increase in the active labor force (some 380,000 persons per
year) requires a net investment of at least — and this seems
ridiculously low — $1.9 billion a year ($5,000 per person)
or a total of $17.1 billion, which is substantially larger than
the level of investment contemplated. In fact, Turkey's
planners anticipate only a gradual reduction in unemployment from 1.5 million in 1962 to perhaps 900,000 in 1967 and
700,000 in 1977. It is admitted that the employment to be
created in industry and services by a 7 per cent growth rate
will not be sufficient to assure the desired distribution of
manpower among the sectors and that unemployment in agriculture will continue. As a matter of fact, because of the
perhaps unrealistically high 7 per cent target, unemployment
can be expected to remain at a much higher level. It is of
course of prime importance to define what is meant by unemployment, and in an underdeveloped economy, almost by
definition, resources are generally underemployed, including human resources. If the potential productive man-hours
not spent in productive labor in Turkey were totaled, the
level of unemployment would undoubtedly rise much higher.

There are many reasons for underemployment. There are
reported to be serious imbalances between the number of
engineers and technicians (a 3:5 ratio) and between doctors and nurses (a 6:1 ratio).[5] (See Table 20.) The engineer
and doctor must thus do the work of technician and nurse.

Such imbalances prevent proper utilization of more highly trained personnel and force them to spend much time in routine activities which could be performed by lesser-trained persons. To this list of imbalances should be added the executive-trained secretary, lawyer-clerk, teacher-assistant, plant manager-foreman ratios.

It may seem somewhat unexpected, but it may well be that the Turkish system is spewing out more skilled labor than can be efficiently organized and supervised, not to mention being supplied with adequate capital equipment with which to use the skills. One bit of evidence to support this observation is the willingness of at least some skilled Turkish labor to work for extended periods of time in western Europe. Possibly 25 per cent of the estimated 200,000 employed in western Europe by mid-1966 were in the skilled labor category (see Tables 31–32). If adequate employment opportunities existed within Turkey, one doubts that there would be this clamor to work in western Europe. Also, note the 94 per cent fulfillment of technical school needs (Table 14).

REGIONAL AND SECTORAL DEMANDS

For reasons already given, one can expect wide variations from region to region in respect to manpower demand, both in amount and quality. Movement is costly in terms of social disorganization and investment in urban facilities. With these facts in mind, some government officials are working toward a policy of (1) discouraging further industrialization in and about congested urban areas by offering incentives to locate elsewhere (such as tax concessions and the establishment of industrial estates) and (2) launching several regional development programs. For some years, the Turkish government has been trying to develop the Erzurum area in the far eastern part of the country, for instance, into an intellectual, entertainment, and industrial center, thereby holding some of the growth element back in its native habitat. More recently the Antalya region of south central Anatolia has received attention, partially under the auspices of the United Nations Special Fund, in that it has been selected as one of the Mediterranean Basin projects. Inventory studies have been carried out, and developmental potentialities calculated. Other regions on which the government is concentrating are those of the eastern Marmara — which is "primarily to solve the economic and social problems of the metropolitan area of Istanbul," [6] the Adana area, and the Zonguldak-Ereğli region, wherein is located Turkey's principal bituminous coal and largest steel enterprises.

Employment in the public sector has been increasing steadily, but at a decreasing rate: from 308,345 in 1955 to 401,179 in 1960, to 403,503 in 1962.[7] The latter figure represented about 15 per cent of total industrial and service employment. In the past, because of the preferred position of state economic enterprise relative to comparable private enterprise, the former has been able to offer fringe benefits of a socially desirable kind to both management and labor. State enterprises were not required to show an internal financial profit and had access to public funds at virtually no interest. Therefore, these enterprises had first call on scarce human resources, the private sector not being able to offer the same financial and social rewards. Since the early years of the Menderes regime, state enterprise has been on a more nearly equal footing with private enterprise, and further moves in the direction of rationalizing state economic enterprise were undertaken following the change of regime in 1960. In the competition for managerial talents, private enterprise seemed to be doing better during the 1955–65 decade. Nonetheless, very substantial latent political power remains in the large state industrial hierarchies, and it is not at all certain that they will remain content to operate on a basis merely competitive with comparable private enterprises. It may develop that once again they will win substantial advantages for themselve. in recruiting scarce human skills, particularly on the professional and managerial level. In the national government sector — excluding state enterprise and local government — there were 268,913 persons employed as of the end of 1964. Some measure of the skills required are reflected in the figures in Table 21. Of the total,

TABLE 21. EDUCATIONAL LEVEL OF NATIONAL GOVERNMENT EMPLOYEES, 1964

Without primary school diploma	32,246
With only primary school diploma	70,459
With middle school diploma	28,119
With lycée diploma	12,248
With vocational school diploma	82,930
With university degree	30,018
Unknown	12,893
TOTAL	268,913

Source: State Statistical Institute, as reported in *Cumhuriyet*, March 27, 1965.

84,111 entered without examination, 79,184 by competitive examination, 19,784 by qualifying examination, and 81,984 by reason of obligatory service arising out of free government training (e.g., teachers).[8]

To achieve the structural changes that Turkish planners envision, the percentage employed in agriculture must be cut from 77 to 58 per cent, while increasing the number in industry from 10 to 15.5 per cent; in services, from 13 to 26 per cent. To correct the present skill imbalances, the number of persons carrying class A skills must be increased from 179,000 in 1965 to 421,000 in 1977; those with class B skills from 177,000 to 570,000; class C from 1,611,000 to 4,560,-

ooo; and class D (excluding agriculture), from 1,693,000 to 2,439,000. During this period, there must be a five-fold increase in the number of teachers (secondary and higher) and technicians; a six-fold increase in auxiliary health personnel (nurses, nurses' aides, midwives, etc.); a four-fold increase in engineers and in foremen. Meanwhile, the number of administrators, entrepreneurs, medical doctors, and primary school teachers is to double. The increase in the number of unskilled workers (non-agricultural) is to be held down to about 50 per cent. Even so, an estimated 700,-ooo will be unemployed in 1977 (perhaps 5 per cent of the labor force). This figure would seem to be unduly optimistic, but the slack may, for political reasons, be taken up by the government sector.

V

HIGH-LEVEL MANPOWER SUPPLY

It is assumed by Turkish planners that educational institutions will be the chief source of supply for high-level manpower.[1] They also assume insignificant emigration. Given the importance of the military in the dissemination of both technical and administrative skills, and the appearance in western Europe by the end of 1965 of some 160,000 Turkish workers[2] (many were skilled or semi-skilled) this may be a grave oversight.[3] Also relevant is the apparent fact that several hundred Turkish medical doctors and scientific personnel have found employment in North America and western Europe. As Turkey integrates more closely with the European Economic Community, the expatriate labor problem may become quite serious. None of these issues are discussed in detail in Turkey's five-year development plan.[4]

SKILLS

Significant ratios in terms of skilled persons/labor force are given in Table 22, followed by the absolute numbers (Table 23) over the past few years.

EDUCATIONAL CAPACITY

The planners have calculated the capacity of Turkey's educational system and the new facilities and teaching staff that will be needed to meet the projected demand. The total number of students believed to be needed in each educa-

TABLE 22. SKILL–LABOR FORCE RATIOS, 1962
(Labor force = 12.7 million in 1962, 15.7 in 1967)

	SKILLED PERSONS		RATIOS	
	1962	1967 EST.	1962	1967 TARGET
Medical doctors	8,900	12,000	7.0/10,000	7.7/10,000
Engineers	12,000	17,000	9.4/10,000	10.8/10,000
Teachers	111,000	160,000	87.4/10,000	101.9/10,000
Lawyers	7,000	na	5.5/10,000	na
Administrators and entrepreneurs	71,000	97,000	55.9/10,000	61.8/10,000
Technicians	142,000	213,000	111.8/10,000	135.7/10,000

Source: Figures adapted from *Five-Year Plan*, pp. 421, 429.
ᵃ Labor force refers to those employed. Estimated unemployed in 1962 was 1.5 million; in 1967, 0.9 million.

tional level and sector in order to meet the demand for skills
is given in Tables 24 and 25. In order to accomplish these
educational objectives, it is estimated that 55.0 per cent of
the 5-to-14 age group must be in school by 1970, 6.0 per cent
of the 15-to-19 age group, 2.0 per cent of the 20-to-24 age
group, or 31.9 per cent of the entire 5-to-24 age group (see
Table 10 for comparison). Comparable U.S. estimates for
1970: 90.0 per cent, 75.0 per cent, 16.0 per cent, 69.4 per
cent.[5] No estimates are given for the flow through the military technical training courses, which is significant.[6]

IMBALANCES

Not given emphasis in the planning — possibly because of
the potentially politically explosive nature of the problem —
is the integration into the manpower development program
of the ethnic and religious minorities and of women. It seems
to be assumed that general development will eliminate these
problems. As already indicated, one may anticipate the
grouping together of the minority groups and of the Turkish
Moslem families, whose women have broken the traditional
restraints, in the big urban centers of Istanbul, Ankara, and
Izmir. Anonymity in a relatively disorganized society may be
equated with greater security for these transitional groups.

TABLE 23. TURKISH SKILLS

	1955	1960	1962
Health			
Medical doctors	7,007	9,826	8,998
Chemists	155	188	211
Pharmacists	1,256	1,406	1,507
Dentists	958	1,395	1,555
Nurses, trained	1,525	2,420	1,564
Midwives	2,001	3,126	3,729
Health officials	3,927	3,890	3,443
	16,799	22,251	21,007
Other professional			
Engineers	7,586	10,977	12,000
Architects	910	na	na
Teachers	58,777	91,229	111,065
Primary school	(42,169)	(65,526)	(75,684)
Others	(16,608)	(25,703)	(35,381)
Lawyers	na	6,393	7,006 (1961)
Administrators and entrepreneurs	na	na	73,000
Technicians	na	na	142,000
Foremen	na	na	50,000
Skilled labor	na	na	686,000
Unskilled labor	na	na	1,326,000
Agriculture (unclassified)	9,446,102	9,737,489	9,860,000

Sources:

Medical, İstatistik, 1960–62, p. 116.

Engineers, Five-Year Plan, p. 421; News from Turkey, March 29, 1956, and August 19, 1959.

Teachers, İstatistik, 1960–62, p. 142.

Lawyers, ibid., p. 178.

Agriculture, 1955–60, İstatistik, 1960–62, p. 81; 1962, Five-Year Plan, p. 421; 1961 figures for administrators and entrepreneurs, professional, technicians, foremen, skilled and unskilled workers, Five-Year Plan, p. 420.

Architects, News from Turkey, March 29, 1956, and August 19, 1959.

Attempts to hold them back in their village or small town environments will probably be futile.

By reference to Tables 22 and 23, it will be noted that Turkey has almost as many lawyers as doctors and that the flow into law continues (see Table 31). The question arises as to whether this represents an optimum allocation of effort. One doubts it. Some type of control will have to be

TABLE 24. NUMBER OF STUDENTS IN VARIOUS EDUCATION BRANCHES
(in thousands)

BRANCH	1962	1963	1964	1965	1966	1967	1972	1977	INDEX 1962 = 100		
									1967	1972	1977
Primary schools	3,367	3,567	3,859	4,141	4,432	4,736	5,992	6,821	141	178	202
Secondary schools	387	387	401	426	455	480	593	641	124	153	166
Lycées	86	96	96	97	102	107	168	204	112	195	237
Technical schools at lycée level	15	17	20	25	30	42	92	126	280	613	840
Vocational lycées (including teachers' training schools)	36	43	53	66	74	81	116	153	225	322	425
Advanced technical education	10	11	13	15	20	27	64	84	270	640	840
General advanced education	51	52	55	57	57	61	116	143	110	227	280

Source: *Five-Year Plan*, p. 424.
Note: On-the-job training and various courses are not included in this table. Information in this respect is given in the relevant sections in the *Five-Year Plan*.

TABLE 25. RATIO OF POPULATION IN THE DIFFERENT EDUCATION BRANCHES TO SCHOOL-AGE POPULATION
(in thousands)

YEARS	PRIMARY EDUCATION			SECONDARY EDUCATION			SCHOOLS OF LYCÉE LEVEL							HIGHER EDUCATION				
							LYCÉE			VOCATIONAL		TECHNICAL			TECHNICAL		GENERAL	
	School-age population (7-12)	Number of students	As % of school-age population	School-age population (13-15)	Number of students	As % of school-age population	School-age population (16-18)	Number of students	As % of school-age population	Number of students	As % of school-age population	Number of students	As % of school-age population	School-age population (19-22)	Number of students	As % of school-age population	Number of students	As % of school-age population
1963	4,480	3,567	73	1,985	387	19.1	1,675	96	5.7	43	2.6	17	1.0	1,880	11	0.6	52	2.7
1964	5,030	3,859	76	2,090	401	19.1	1,770	96	5.4	53	2.9	20	1.1	1,940	13	0.7	55	2.8
1965	5,150	4,141	80	2,200	427	19.0	1,870	97	5.2	66	3.5	25	1.3	2,040	15	0.7	57	2.7
1966	5,270	4,432	84	2,300	455	19.7	1,970	102	5.2	74	3.8	30	1.5	2,150	20	0.9	57	2.6
1967	5,390	4,736	87	2,390	480	20.0	2,075	107	5.2	81	3.9	42	1.9	2,275	27	1.2	61	2.7
1972	5,990	5,990	100	2,715	593	21.9	2,520	168	6.7	116	4.6	92	3.6	2,950	64	2.2	116	3.9
1977	6,820	6,820	100	3,000	641	20.1	2,800	204	7.3	153	5.5	126	4.5	3,450	84	2.4	143	4.1

Source: *Five-Year Plan*, p. 424.

instituted over entry into traditionally high-prestige professions that are of a lesser value to development than perhaps others. But recent enrollment figures do not reflect such controls, subtle or otherwise. The only universities that seem consciously to have devised long-range plans related to the projections of manpower needs made by the government are the Middle East Technical University and the newly-established Haccetepe Science Center. Curiously, both are relatively new and both are more insulated from direct state control than are the other institutions of higher learning.

Another supply imbalance is reflected in the Turkish Ministry of Education report of 1963 in which a severe shortage of teachers in the primary and secondary school systems is emphasized. At that time, the qualifications and numbers of primary school teachers were those indicated in Table 26.

TABLE 26. QUALIFICATIONS OF PRIMARY SCHOOL TEACHERS, 1963

Qualified regular teachers	53,194
Regular teachers assigned to teaching during the period of military service	649
Reserve officers other than trained teachers assigned to teaching during their period of compulsory military service	8,079
Temporary teachers	5,971
Acting temporary teachers	5,034
Instructors	2,640
TOTAL	75,576

Source: "Report on Developments in Education During the 1962–63 School Year" (Turkish Ministry of Education, 1963, presented to the XXVI Educational Conference in Geneva, July 1963), p. 6.

The same source reported a concurrent shortage of 12,310 teachers in the secondary schools. The demand was there, but not the supply.

In order to fill the vacancies in the primary and secondary school system and to improve teaching competency, the following moves were anticipated in mid-1963:[7]

1. Enlarge existing normal schools.
2. Set up new teacher training schools.
3. Enlist university graduates.
4. Encourage and help secondary school graduates to take the teaching certificate examination.
5. Train lycée and normal school graduates as secondary school teachers.
6. Train secondary school graduates in special courses as temporary teachers (4,500 had been so trained in summer courses by mid-1963) and help them prepare for the regular teaching certificate examination.
7. Enlist the services of reserve army officers as teachers.
8. Postpone the military service of teachers until the age of 31.
9. Recruit temporary acting teachers from different sources.
10. Give primary school teachers the opportunity to take the required course examination of pedagogical institutions without attending school and thus qualify as secondary school teachers.
11. Institute summer training sessions at the universities and pedagogical institutions to permit completion of higher teacher training.
12. Require all primary education teachers to attend refresher courses provided locally in the summer (under a 1961 law) by the In-service Education Bureau.

Given Turkey's 1962 resources of skills and the projected output of the educational program, 1963–1967, Turkey's planners derived the manpower supply estimates shown in Table 22. It will be noted that in comparison with Tables 20 and 23, at least two important inexplicable discrepancies appear for 1962: the number of health personnel (other than doctors) and primary school teachers.

ON-THE-JOB TRAINING

In addition to the output of the formal education system, training programs in industry are expected to supply the bulk of the increase in skilled workers. For example, note that of the expected increase of 50,000 between 1963 and 1964, 35,000 are to be trained in industry. Of the 5,000 increase in foremen over the same period, 3,500 are to be produced by industry itself (see Table 27). In implementing the

TABLE 27. PERSONNEL TO BE TRAINED IN INDUSTRY

YEARS	FOREMEN	SKILLED WORKERS
1963	3,500	35,000
1964	3,500	35,000
1965	4,200	41,000
1966	4,900	48,000
1967	5,600	55,000
1968–1972	40,000	360,000
1973–1977	80,000	660,000

Source: *Five-Year Plan,* p. 425.

Vocational Centers Project, a part of the general development plan, 114 training units will have been established in various industries by 1967. Six-month courses are planned, and an annual output of 3,300 persons from 1968 onward is expected.[8]

Overlooked in the financial manpower development programs is the relevancy of the military establishment. Although information on the military educational system is scanty, many thousands of young men receive general education and technical training in military schools each year. If the annual draft class approximates 200,000, at least half of these would receive training that upgrades their economically-valuable skills to a significant extent during the subsequent two years they are in military service. In addition, the officer corps, probably numbering about 40,000 men, is a source of much of Turkey's high-level administrative talent, both for the private and public sectors. A recent statement by one of Turkey's top generals points out that the officer corps comprises the "largest group of enlightened men in the country." He also observed that especially in the past few years officers had been needed in civilian services, presumably in teaching and government administration.[9]

On the supply side, the high-level manpower problem can be broken down briefly to: (1) diversion of more people into high priority vocations despite traditional prestige patterns (which were perhaps once functional but, due to rapid change, are no longer so), (2) attracting the more creative — not simply the more intelligent — groups into high-level institutions of learning, and (3) preventing an out-migration of those with valuable skills. In the final analysis, a nation's growth rests on the *creatively-minded* individuals who have acquired sufficient knowledge and skills to innovate, and *who remain at home.*

It might seem practical for the optimum use of human resources that a real effort should be made to pull into the high-level manpower category those people disposed to be creative. Who are they? It can be assumed they are those who are denied expected status in traditional society because of externally-induced changes — such as the displacement of religious authority, or the displacement of small landowners from the rural scene. Emigré labor, and lycée and university students of village origin, may be highly creative groups, also the new urban dwellers of Shiite religious identification, as well as those of Kurdish ethnic extraction. It is also possible that women will play a special role.

VI

THE PROCESS OF
HUMAN CAPITAL FORMATION

FORMAL EDUCATIONAL SYSTEM

The base of Turkey's educational system is a free, five-year primary school, attendance at which is legally compulsory for those between seven and twelve years of age. However, some 15,636 villages had no access to a school as of the beginning of 1964.[1] And it was stated officially that at the beginning of the 1964 school year primary school capacity was deficient by 920,000 places.[2] In addition, some 2,000 village schools were of the three-year variety, in which the instructor was not a properly qualified teacher. The inadequacy of the basic school system was also reflected in the fact that although there was a flow of 400,000 graduates out of the five-year primary school in June 1964, the input capacity of the middle schools (and vocational schools of similar level) was only 140,000.[3] As a matter of fact, although gaining steadily, still only slightly over 40 per cent of the primary school graduates are moving on into grade 6 in the middle school (see Chart IV and Table 28). It is also to be noted that the drop-out rate for girls is almost twice the rate for boys.

Of the 971 middle schools in 1962–63,[4] all but a handful were located in towns and cities, and none in the villages other than a few of the very largest ones in the western part

TABLE 28. PERCENTAGE OF PRIMARY SCHOOL GRADUATES WHO ENTERED
MIDDLE AND VOCATIONAL SCHOOLS

YEAR	PRIMARY SCHOOL GRADUATES		ENTERED MIDDLE SCHOOLS (Columns 3 over 1, 4 over 2)		ENTERED MIDDLE SCHOOL-LEVEL VOCATIONAL SCHOOLS	
	Boys (1)	Girls (2)	Boys (3)	Girls (4)	Boys (5)	Girls (6)
1934–35	20,120	8,293				
1935–36			72.1%	67.0%	5.93%	7.30%
1944–45	66,244	23,499				
1945–46			21.2	25.0	22.3	10.3
1950–51	102,384	42,476				
1951–52			21.9	15.7	6.67	6.24
1958–59	177,992	88,810[a]				
1959–60	(193,847)	(95,825)[b]	42.6 (39.4)	27.2 (25.2)	4.00	6.50
1960–61[c]	226,280	111,474				
1961–62			50.8	28.8	?	?

Sources: Reshat Özalp, *Türkiyede Meslekî ve Teknik Öğretim* (Ankara: Maarif Basımevi, 1956), pp. 15–19. T. C. Millî Eğitim Bakanliği, *Meslekî ve Teknik Öğretim Müesseseriyle Ilgili Rakamlar* (Ankara: Bengi Matbassï, 1961), p. 18. The figures given by the various sources vary. According to those of the technical and vocational branch of the Ministry in 1959–60, the percentages of those who entered *ORTA* schools were for boys 45.1% and for girls 24.7%. The figures for the years after 1958 were computed from statistics of the Research and Measurement Bureau of the Ministry of Education. Adapted from Kazamias, "Education and the Quest for Modernity in Turkey," Table VIII, p. 324.
[a] Those who received diplomas.
[b] Those who enrolled in the fifth class.
[c] Enrollment in public primary schools.

of the country. Clearly, the big hurdle in the Turkish educational system still lies between the primary and secondary schools. If a student reaches grade 6 (first year in middle school), there is an excellent chance that he will continue into a lycée (grades 9–11) or into a lycée-level vocational school (see Table 29). If in a lycée, the student has a 4 out of 5 chance of going on into higher education of some sort (see Table 30).

In the interest of high-level manpower development, need the flow be stepped up between the primary and secondary levels? It should be borne in mind that a very large proportion of the more creative persons, the raw material for the

TABLE 29. PERCENTAGE OF MIDDLE (*ORTA*) SCHOOL GRADUATES
WHO ENTERED LYCÉE AND VOCATIONAL/TECHNICAL SCHOOLS

YEAR	MIDDLE SCHOOL GRADUATES		ENTERED LYCÉE (Columns 3 over 1, 4 over 2)		ENTERED POST MIDDLE SCHOOL VOCATIONAL AND TECHNICAL SCHOOLS	
	Boys (1)	Girls (2)	Boys (3)	Girls (4)	Boys (5)	Girls (6)
1934–35	5,589	1,877				
1935–36			79.2%	66.2%	17.4%	38.0%
			(4,428)	(1,244)	(976)	(526)
1939–40	10,397	3,878				
1940–41			48.3	39.9	9.2	15.6
			(5,029)	(1,548)	(960)	(607)
1944–45	10,391	3,356				
1945–46			46.5	38.1	22.1	43.1
			(4,728)	(1,279)	(2,302)	(1,449)
1949–50	7,864	2,990				
1950–51			61.9	42.4	21.2	45.8
			(4,873)	(1,268)	(1,667)	(1,373)
1954–55	12,648	4,411	60.5	41.8	17.1	16.4
			(7,650)	(1,843)	(2,158)	(725)
1958–59	24,656	8,281	51.6	48.8	24.4	20.4
			(12,711)	(4,038)	(6,012)	(1,687)

Source: Özalp, *Mesleki ve Teknik Öğretim,* p. 18. Taken from Kazamias, "Education and the Quest for Modernity in Turkey," Table IX, p. 325.

embodiment of high-level skills, are already in an urban setting where adequate primary schools exist, but not secondary. And most of the women who might move on to the subprofessional level, if given adequate education, are likewise in the cities. The point is that those with the psychological set that could equip them for the most productive use of high-level skills are not remaining in the rural and small town environment where traditional society still dominates.

A specially appointed National Education Commission (1959), on which a number of outstanding Turkish educators sat, cast doubt on the social and economic value of five years of primary education which had no follow-up. As already noted, relatively few village children were finding their way into a secondary school, virtually all of which were located in the towns, and few village parents seemed to see

TABLE 30. DISTRIBUTION OF STUDENTS BY TYPE OF SCHOOL
(Percentage enrolled in various types of school)

YEAR	PRIMARY	MIDDLE	LYCÉE	TECHNICAL/ VOCATIONAL (middle and lycée level)	HIGHER (post-lycée)	UNIVERSITIES ONLY
1932–33	89.5%	7.5%	1.6%	.5%	.9%	
1935–36	98.3	7.4	1.8	.6	.8	(included in
1940–41	86.1	9.5	2.3	.8	1.2	"Higher"
1945–46	89.2	5.6	1.8	2.1	1.3	category)
1948–49	89.3	5.0	1.5	2.6	1.6	
1961–62	84.5	8.5	2.2	2.9	1.9	1.2

Source: Richard D. Robinson, "An Analysis of Turkish Education," (Ankara: IBRD, a working paper for the 1950 Economic Survey Mission to Turkey, 1950), p. 20. The figures for 1961–62 were taken from tabulations furnished by the Research and Measurement Bureau (mimeographed). Adapted from Kazamias, "Education and the Quest for Modernity in Turkey," Table X, p. 326.

the value of secondary education, particularly for girls, nor could they spare their children's labor at the times of peak load (harvest, sowing, cultivation). Neither did they feel that they had the cash to provide board and room while their children attended a town school, only a fortunate few having town-dwelling relatives willing to assume responsibility. Also, in the typical village there was virtually no juvenile literature which would encourage children to continue reading after graduation from fifth grade. Under these conditions, it was suspected that effective literacy was lost by most children within three to five years after primary school graduation.

By 1960, the army was lending its enormous prestige to further basic education, thereby increasing popular acceptance of, if not demand for, education. The army set up sixteen basic education centers at which all illiterate draftees, an estimated 50 per cent, were required to attend a four-month course. From 1960 to 1962, inclusive, 155,000 men moved through these courses. The present capacity is 49,200 students per year. Their study focuses on acquiring literacy, simple arithmetic skills, the concept of measuring, plus some exposure to hygiene and Turkish history. For illiterates, the normal two-year period of compulsory military service has been lengthened by four months to accommodate this new training, with a two-month reduction for successful completion of the literacy course. Special books, deemed to be of interest to soldiers, have been printed for free distribution, the purpose of which was to stimulate the habit of reading and to develop reading skills. But this program did not touch the female population, and the problem of the secondary school remained.[5]

The 1959 National Education Commission recommended a slowdown in the construction of new village primary schools (about half of the villages had one by 1960) and more emphasis on secondary schools to service rural areas.

The authors of the 1962–67 plan, however, moved in the other direction and set as a target 100 per cent primary school attendance by 1972.[6] One problem the Commission saw was that the village communities were too small to justify separate secondary schools, and the cost and the difficulty of transportation rendered regional schools unrealistic in most areas. The Commission also urged that differences between rural and city schools be narrowed so as to avoid the creation of two distinct educational systems within the country.

Under the Village Institute system, which was modified subsequent to the 1950 change of regime, the type of education offered in the villages had been quite different from that given in the towns, which made it even more difficult for the village children to move on into the secondary school system, even if they or their parents so desired, which few did. As other forms of practical education were extended into the villages, such as mobile units teaching practical skills, the farm machinery schools, the agricultural extension service, and military technical training, the type of practical training formerly stimulated by the Village Institute system was perhaps no longer necessary. There began to be more emphasis on turning out village teachers better equipped to teach basic cultural subjects. For several years, the Village Institutes have been called simply "Primary Teachers Training Schools," and there has been an attempt to enroll in them at least a minimum of teacher trainees of city or town origin. The authorities felt that by mixing village and town youth in this fashion, the enormous difference between country and city mentality might be narrowed. But in practice, it proved virtually impossible to attract any significant number of town and city youth into the village teaching program.

The findings of Bradburn's 1959 research in Turkey "indicated that cultural value-orientation centering around concern with the present to the exclusion of planning for the future and a non-activist approach to the environment and a consequent low need for achievement [were] . . . the major non-economic forces retarding economic development in Turkey." [7] Though he felt that the overwhelmingly dominant role of the father in the Turkish family tended to block rapid increase in achievement motivation, still he found some evidence of change. He speculated that this increase in achievement motivation was possibly a product of the Primary Teachers Training Schools, various adult training programs, the rapid growth of cities and consequent geographical separation of families, and even the primary and secondary schools themselves. He reported that in a world sample of stories from third and fourth grade readers, those from Turkey contained "the highest degree of achievement imaginary," which was taken as indicating that Turkish educators were concerned with "instilling achievement values." [8] Bradburn might have added to his list of forces eroding the dominance of the father two more: (1) the impact of two years of military training in a modern army, and (2) the weakening of religious justification for the traditional pattern of family relations. There has been some talk recently of reconstituting the Village Institutes as Village Development Institutes, but this effort seems to have been blocked.

The most recent move at the elementary school level to modernize instruction is the introduction of "progressive education." What is meant by this term is a research and problem-solving approach, oriented toward the individual student, within a more simplified curriculum which at least in part is determined by the teacher. Emphasis is to be placed on the value and uniqueness of the individual. In 1963–64, the system was tried experimentally in a few selected urban schools, and in 1964–65 in several hundred schools. In 1967 the system is to be extended to all elementary schools, rural and urban. Meanwhile, summer seminars for teachers and school inspectors are being held to educate them in the new method.[9]

In the 1967–68 school year, all graduates of middle schools enrolled in institutes of fine arts, technical schools, commercial lycées, and schools for religious leaders (*imam ve hatip*) will be given the opportunity to take a special examination. Those who perform satisfactorily will win the right to enter a university or higher school as do graduates of the regular lycée. Another innovation is the introduction in the primary schools of an initial ungraded two-year period. Whenever the student is ready, he will be passed into the third grade. In the third year, satisfactory performance will pass the child into the fourth grade. In the fifth grade, he will be given a primary-school graduation examination. Those who fail to pass will be given an intensive 15-day course and given a second opportunity. These moves are designed to stimulate the flow of students through the educational system and thereby make it more efficient.[10]

Turkish educational planners, as educational planners else-

where, have failed to make explicit a number of their assumptions. Chief among them is that the 11- or 12-year pre-
college program is a valid one. The relevant question: Is
commencement of formal education at age 5 or 6 optimum
in the Turkish situation? It might be more efficient, in terms
of the ratio between resource input and socially valuable
educational output, to start formal education later, say at
age 15 or 16, and compress the entire content of the pre-
college curriculum into 5 or 6 years. Life expectancy at age
15 is likely to be substantially greater than at age 5 or 6 in
a country such as Turkey. Also, at this age, aptitude and
motivation testing are perhaps more accurate. And finally,
literacy gained at this age might be retained more readily
even though the individual were exposed to no further formal education. It is very doubtful that a very large percentage of the children dropping out of the school system at the
end of primary school (at age 10 or 11) retain literacy into
adulthood. By contrast, in some more developed societies,
formal education should perhaps commence earlier, say at
age 4, the relevant variables being life expectancy at various
ages, degree of harmony between home and school and community environments, and the drop-out rates at various educational levels. At the very least, these questions should be
investigated and not assumed to be universally valid in the
sense of being optimum under all conditions.

The entire primary and secondary school system (diagrammed in Chart VI) is under the direct supervision of the
Ministry of Education, which makes coordinated educational
planning somewhat easier than would otherwise be the case.
No private school may operate in Turkey without the specific approval of the Ministry and unless it conforms to rather
elaborate regulations issued by the Ministry. In 1962–63,
some 27,000 primary students (out of a total of 3.4 million),
18,000 middle school students (out of 355,000), and 11,000

CHART VI. ORGANIZATIONAL DIAGRAM OF TURKISH PUBLIC SCHOOLS, 1961–1962

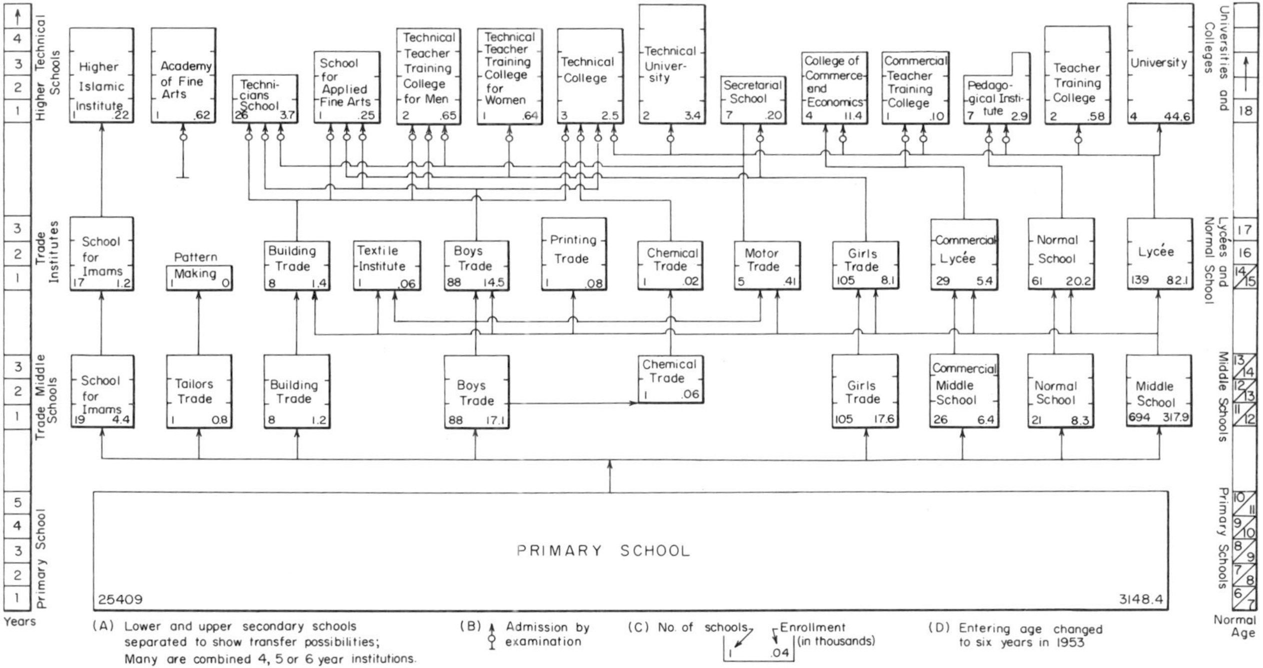

Source: Turkish Ministry of Education, Educational Research and Evaluation Center, Ankara, 1962.

lycée students (out of 104,000) were enrolled in private schools, including a handful of minority and foreign-sponsored schools. Being centrally controlled — including school construction and the assignment and payment of teachers — the public schools are not generally supported by any direct *local* participation.

Paralleling the central core of regular middle and lycée schools are technical and vocational schools of comparable levels in commerce, fine arts, public health, industrial arts, home economics, agriculture, military, and teaching (see Charts VII and VIII). Lying academically just above the high schools or lycées, of which there were 215 in the 1962–63 school year and which are situated only in the larger cities and towns, are the so-called "higher schools." These are vocationally oriented and include schools of dentistry, merchant marine, pharmacy, fine arts, commerce, music, journalism, and pedagogy. Also included in this category is the American-sponsored Robert College in Istanbul which offers degrees in liberal arts, business and economics, and engineering.

There is evidence that private lycée graduates seeking admission to the universities have, as a group, scored higher on entrance examinations than public lycée graduates, particularly in foreign languages (which could be expected in that the teaching medium in some of these schools is a foreign language). Of the ten highest scoring lycée groups, five were from private, and five from public, schools. Since there were at that time (1960) 58 private and 134 public lycées, the result was much in favor of the former.[11] Andreas M. Kazamias found a higher percentage (25.4) of private lycée students with professional fathers than those in public lycées (11.6).[12] It would appear that those with the necessary wealth to afford a private lycée education have a much better chance of gaining admission to higher education, which fact

CHART VII. THE TURKISH EDUCATIONAL SYSTEM
(i.e., those schools related to the Ministry of Education)

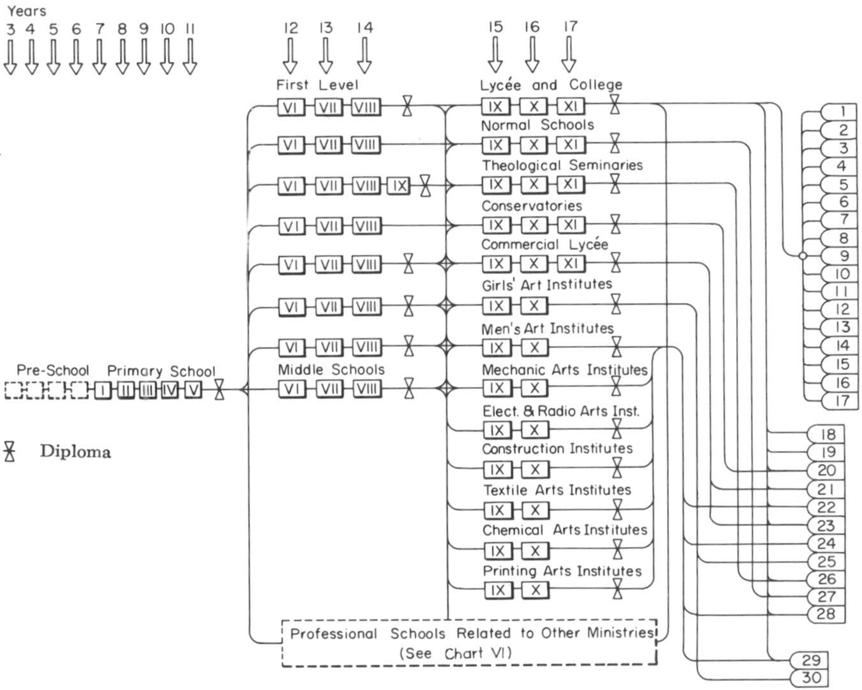

Years
3 4 5 6 7 8 9 10 11

12 13 14   15 16 17

First Level   Lycée and College

Normal Schools

Theological Seminaries

Conservatories

Commercial Lycée

Girls' Art Institutes

Men's Art Institutes

Mechanic Arts Institutes

Elect. & Radio Arts Inst.

Construction Institutes

Textile Arts Institutes

Chemical Arts Institutes

Printing Arts Institutes

Middle Schools

Pre-School   Primary School

⋈ Diploma

Professional Schools Related to Other Ministries
(See Chart VI)

1. Literature Faculty
2. Language, History, Geography Faculty
3. Science Faculty
4. Law Faculty
5. Divinity Faculty
6. Political Science Faculty
7. Medical Faculty
8. Veterinary Faculty
9. Agriculture Faculty
10. Forestry Faculty
11. Economics Faculty
12. Mining and Engineering Faculty
13. Civil Engineering Faculty
14. Electrical Engineering Faculty
15. Architecture Faculty
16. Mechanical Engineering Faculty
17. Administrative Science Faculty
18. Advanced Normal School
19. Fine Arts Academy
20. State Conservatory
21. Economics and Commercial Science Academy
22. Technical School
23. Advanced Commercial Normal School
24. Men's Technical Normal School
25. Women's Technical Normal School
26. Advanced Islamic Institute
27. Educational Institute
28. Practical Arts School
29. Technical Schools
30. Secretarial School
31. Primary and Middle Art Institute, Technical Schools and similar Institutions

Source: M. Nuri Kodamoğlu, *Türkiyede Eğitim* (Ankara: Millî Eğitim Basîmevi, 1965), fig. 1.

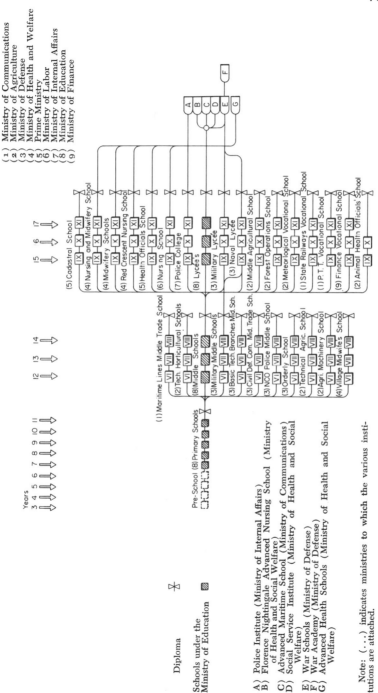

CHART VIII. TURKISH SCHOOLS RELATED TO VARIOUS MINISTRIES

(1) Ministry of Communications
(2) Ministry of Agriculture
(3) Ministry of Defense
(4) Ministry of Health and Welfare
(5) Prime Ministry
(6) Ministry of Labor
(7) Ministry of Internal Affairs
(8) Ministry of Education
(9) Ministry of Finance

Diploma ⊁

Schools under the Ministry of Education ▨

A) Police Institute (Ministry of Internal Affairs)
B) Florence Nightingale Advanced Nursing School (Ministry of Health and Social Welfare)
C) Advanced Maritime School (Ministry of Communications)
D) Social Service Institute (Ministry of Health and Social Welfare)
E) War Schools (Ministry of Defense)
F) War Academy (Ministry of Defense)
G) Advanced Health Schools (Ministry of Health and Social Welfare)

Note: (...) indicates ministries to which the various institutions are attached.

Source: M. Nuri Kodamoğlu, *Türkiyede Eğitim* (Ankara: Millî Eğitim Basımevi, 1964), fig. 2.

undoubtedly exaggerates the already present "opportunity gap" between elite and mass and blocks university admission for many of the more dynamic youth found among the poorer and newer urban dwellers. The move to break through the wall between those in regular lycées and those in lycée vocational schools in respect to university admission, already mentioned, is a step in this direction.

At the top of the academic pyramid (excluding the armed service academies) are seven universities, all of which enjoy a semi-autonomous position but derive funds from annual parliamentary appropriations. The seven, with their constituent faculties and 1963 student enrollments, are: .

Ankara University (Ankara, 17,441 students in 1962–63): law, political science, language — history — geography, science, medicine, theology, pharmacy, veterinary medicine, agriculture.

Atatürk University (Erzurum, 1,038 students): science — literature, agriculture.

Istanbul University (Istanbul, 25,013 students): literature, science, law, economics, medicine, forestry, plus institutes of management and of journalism.

Aegean University (Izmir, 1,235 students): medicine, agriculture, science.

Middle East Technical University (Ankara, 1,038 students): science — literature, administrative science, engineering, architecture.

Haccetepe Science Center (Ankara, newly established): medicine, arts and sciences, nursing, agriculture (located in Erzurum), graduate.

At least two additional universities are soon to make their appearance.

The Middle East Technical University, now in its ninth year and founded with United Nations Special Fund assistance, was designed to be of a regional nature, pulling students from all of the Middle Eastern countries. Supported in part by the Turkish government, it enjoys a semi-autonomous position. About 10 per cent of its student body is from other Middle Eastern countries. Unlike the other Turkish universities, the medium of instruction is primarily English. An enrollment of 6,000 is expected by 1967.[13] The breakdown by faculties, including all universities other than Haccetepe, plus the higher vocational schools, is given in Table 31. Not included are the military schools.

TABLE 31. COLLEGE ENROLLMENT IN TURKEY

NUMBER IN:	1955	1960	1962
Law	12,173	14,531	15,888
Political, admin., commercial science	694	1,255	1,304
Liberal arts	2,462	8,285	9,266
Science	3,275	5,253	5,958
Medicine	3,345	4,369	4,147
Theology	83	230	268
Pharmacy	217	530	875
Veterinary medicine	468	587	408
Horticulture	888	2,044	2,273
Engineering	2,251	3,066	2,223
Architecture	—	123	158
Economics	2,154	3,665	3,760
Forestry	183	953	1,034
Maritime	152	223	193
Dentistry	393	378	385
Fine arts	421	634	973
Education	1,005	2,944	3,775
Journalism	209	466	406
Other college level	1,662	4,914	6,494

Source: İstatistik, 1960–62, pp. 169–172.

Finally, there is a constant stream of Turkish students going off in search of education abroad. By the last count available (1959–60), this group totaled 3,017 (excluding military trainees), of which 1,543 were in Germany, 815 in the United States, 118 in France, 136 in Switzerland, 130 in the United Kingdom, 40 in Italy, and 235 elsewhere. About 14 per cent of these were on government scholarships.[14]

ADULT EDUCATION

In addition there are a variety of adult education programs, including a number of night schools, several "Courses" given by traveling cadres of instructors (subjects include village metalworking and carpentry, construction and forestry, village women's sewing) and the so-called "People's Classrooms." Peace Corp volunteers are now being assigned to some of these cadres, whose students are primarily village adults.

In this connection, the "people's education" (*halk eğitim*) programs of the newly founded Ministry of Rural Affairs should be mentioned. One of these is the encouragement of village school teachers to offer courses to village adults in reading and writing, arithmetic, or Turkish history. A minimum of ten students must sign up. The teacher receives an additional monthly stipend for his efforts. However, if the number of students falls below ten during the year, the course is closed and the teacher receives no stipend. In one quite progressive province, 121 such courses were given in the 1961–62 school year, all but 12 being in the villages and small towns. Due to the fact that some of the teachers were not paid as promised, the number of courses dropped and, in 1962–63, only 15 were given. Presumably these courses are organized on three levels: A for illiterates, B for literates, C for the more advanced. A primary diploma is not given. Activity of this sort, plus the current program to establish reading rooms in a large number of villages, is the responsibility of the Adult Education Director, who is a member of the staff of the provincial governor and is equal in rank to the Director of Public Education on the provincial level.

Another adult educational effort in Turkey merits comment, although it is at present not a vital force. Reference is to the People's Houses, the *Halk Evi,* established by the Republican People's Party in 1930 as local adult education and cultural centers. During their heyday a People's House was found in virtually every provincial center and important town in Turkey and housed libraries, small theaters, and various other cultural and vocational facilities. During the latter years of the Republican People's Party regime (1945–50), the People's Houses became centers of partisan political activity, so much so that in some instances the local party headquarters was found in the People's House. In addition, the party not infrequently compelled the local government to allocate public funds for the maintenance of these centers. Consequently, as the People's Party became discredited during its final years in power, this discredit also tarnished the image of the People's Houses. And when, in 1950, the Democratic Party came to power, the People's Houses were abolished by act of law. Unfortunately, they have not been replaced by any nonpartisan centers except where local groups have seen fit to seize the initiative. There is no doubt that this institution came out of a deliberate effort on the part of Turkey's first president, Mustafa Kemal Atatürk, to stimulate and encourage the more creative and progressive elements in the provincial towns. The centers also, of course, provided a mechanism through which the central government could communicate effectively with these local growth elements. In some areas, to my personal knowledge, the People's Houses became important centers of local cultural activity. They also served in some instances as important centers for local research into regional folklore and, hence, helped create and sustain the new Turkish nationalism. These institutions are being reconstituted as essentially non-partisan, local cultural associations joined in a very loose national federation with but token financial support from public sources.

MILITARY EDUCATIONAL SYSTEM AND MANPOWER
DEVELOPMENT EFFORTS

The largest number of students to go abroad has probably been in the military category, although figures have not been published in recent years. Because of the important role that the military establishment plays in the development of high-level technical and managerial manpower in Turkey, a description of the military educational system is in order.

Since 1950, five institutions have been connected with the Commandant of the War Academy: the Army Academy; the Air Force Academy; the Naval Academy; the Joint Staff Academy; and the Academy of National Defense. Those officers who finish two years in the Army, Naval, or Air Academy then enter the Joint Staff Academy for one year of training for general staff duty. The Academy of National Defense is designed to give further training to officers of field or general rank with the objective of strengthening the cooperation between the civilian and military authorities and to give further training in the mobilization of the country's resources in time of emergency. Underlying these academies is a system of military lycées, for which the number of applicants has been increasing in recent years. But again there are no published statistics. The curriculum in these schools differs from those in the normal lycées by the addition of more applied courses and a number designed to teach mechanical skills. Graduates of the staff college, or the Joint Staff Academy, are known as *kurmay subaylar*, or staff officers, whether or not they are serving in a staff capacity.

All three branches of the service also maintain reserve officers' schools, into which qualified lycée graduates are accepted. At the end of their training in these schools, they are commissioned as second lieutenants in their respective branches. In addition, of course, all branches maintain a large number of technical training schools for both officers and enlisted men. For instance, the air force maintains a war school, a reserve officer school, a technical school, a communications school, a supply school and a maintenance school. The list of army training schools, many of which are located in or about Ankara, include those for veterinary medicine, cartography, communications, personnel, music, medicine, cavalry, engineering, supply, finance, and artillery. As of mid-1956, the number of officers, both on active and inactive duty (including reservists), was reported to have been as follows: army, 102,897; navy, 56,480; air force, 138,-850; marines, 12,593. No more recent figures have been published.

Until the change of regime in 1950 and subsequent military reforms (in part instituted by reason of American insistence), it was impossible for a noncommissioned officer to move into the commissioned officer rank. Later, a change in regulations made such vertical movement possible, although it would appear that, in fact, very few noncommissioned officers have broken through. Also, prior to the reforms of the 1950's, any lycée graduate could secure entry into the reserve officer corps. Although a lycée degree is still normally required, a lycée graduate is not now assured an officer's commission. In these ways, the previous Prussian-like system operating in the Turkish army has been broken and promotion placed more on the basis of achievement and demonstrated ability rather than on certain ascriptive qualities and sheer seniority. It is doubtful that non-Turkish and non-Moslem elements, such as Kurds and Shiites, are represented in the officer corps in proportion to their numbers.

Virtually every young man finishes his compulsory two-year service in the army with some mechanical skill and the desire to acquire more. In addition, a large number of foremen are originating in the army's noncommissioned officer corps, which group consisted of an estimated 60,000 in 1960. Insofar as is known, no statistical studies have been made of this flow, but casual observation has convinced this author that such a sequence is not uncommon. It should be pointed out further that the achievement of noncommissioned officer status in the Turkish army carries with it substantial prestige. For example, an individual returning to his village or small town, having achieved the rank of a sergeant, will be called sergeant so-and-so the rest of his life. Although both the school and the army are hammering away at traditional society, the army's impact is possibly the more significant because it removes the youth from his own environment entirely and thrusts him into a world where what a person knows and can do is all important, not who he is. Making the process more effective is a deliberate policy of assigning village youth to town and city and the reverse.

It is difficult to derive any exact measure of the flow through the various military training establishments which have relevancy to useful civilian skills. A rough partial estimate based on the 1964–65 training plan for the Turkish ground forces appears in Table 32.

What a person knows and can do may be broken down into four elements: psychological (motivation, receptivity, self-identity), mental (intelligence), motor (skills), physical (health, or energy level). The army draftee undergoes change in all four dimensions, even in intelligence as defined by testing. The accomplishment of literacy by an adult seems, according to tests given in the Turkish army, to have a significant impact on his general alertness, ability to analyze problems, and capacity to learn new skills. Bear in mind that in traditional Turkish society military service has been equivalent to formal initiation into manhood. If there is validity in Daniel Lerner's thesis that physical mobility is

TABLE 32. PARTIAL ESTIMATE OF THOSE RECEIVING TECHNICAL TRAINING
WITH CIVILIAN APPLICATION IN THE TURKISH ARMY, 1964–1965

Vehicle repairs	3,150	Telephone repairs	96
Radio repairs	600	Teletypewriters	192
Radio operators	1,770	Photo lab technicians	96
Drivers	11,300	Linemen	96
Welders	450	Draftsmen	48
Grader operators	189	Boat maintenance	40
Tractor operators	81	Office machine maintenance	15
Compressor operators	39	Refrigeration specialists	8
Crane operators	182	Dental technicians	30
Heavy equipment mechanics	239	Medical lab technicians	15
Power unit operators	609	Pharmacy technicians	18
General utility repairs	304	Medical aidmen	600
Switchboard operators	90	TOTAL	20,257

Source: "Enlisted Men Specialist and Troop NCO Courses Program for
1964–1965" (Ankara: Ministry of National Defense, 1964. Mimeographed).

related to psychic mobility, then the army-forced movement
of young men into new physical environments induces a
subtle psychological change that tends to transform the individual from a traditionalist to a transitionalist.[15] The individual is then psychologically equipped to acquire new skills,
undertake new jobs, and participate in a new pattern of social relationships. Accelerated economic development, which
is the goal of the Turkish elite, requires parallel social development, and that requires almost a discontinuity between
generations. The military is contributing substantially to this
process, and doing so quite deliberately.[16]

The army has undertaken several programs to stimulate
manpower development other than its own internal training
effort. In 1962, the National Security Council issued a directive to use the capabilities and resources of the armed forces,
short of impeding their combat effectiveness, for the implementation of the five-year plan. Specifically listed were these
activities: reforestation, medical services for nearby communities, agricultural pest and disease control, civilian pro-

duction in the military factories, water exploration, airport construction, dredging, civilian research, and rural education.[17] To give some cohesiveness to such projects, the "sister village" (*kardeş köy*) concept emerged. Each army unit, headquarters and separate establishment was authorized to designate any village within 15 kilometers of their respective garrisons as a sister village. Assistance was to be on a voluntary basis, and to continue for at least one year and not more than two. The selection of more than a single village in each case was authorized only after the first had reached a desirable level of development. Assistance was to be given in: (1) donations of money, material and clothing by members of the units and their families; (2) the construction of schools, fountains, water supply systems, sewers, illumination facilities; (3) medical aid in the form of provision of physical examinations by military medical personnel and emergency evacuation to hospitals; (4) veterinary aid in hygiene and inoculations, (5) agricultural matters and in the case of natural disasters, (6) invitations to village representatives to the unit day or other celebrations, (7) the showing of educational films, (8) the encouragement of athletic events. The Sister Village project went into effect as of August 30, 1964, and by the end of 1964 the army had selected 566 villages; the navy, 31; and the air force, 53.[18] According to a press account, in one small area of Turkey, by the end of 1964, local military units had planted 750,000 trees, and in "sister villages" had constructed three new schools, and repaired 82 more, had constructed three reading rooms, had taught 30 village children to read, had given 25 scholarships to poor villagers, and had distributed books and teaching materials to over 100 village schools. In addition, military doctors had conducted clinics and distributed medicines in the villages.[19]

By October 1964, one army spokesman could report that

in each garrison, fifty needy students per regiment had been clothed, the selection of these students having been made by the school administration on the basis of good conduct, hard work, and other related factors. And in garrisons where no lycées existed, transportation facilities used by the children of military personnel were likewise made available for a certain number of selected needy village children who otherwise would not have been able to continue their education.[20]

In mid-1965, one unusually perceptive officer pointed out publicly that with a little planning, the army could become even more effective as an instrument of change and manpower development. He urged that men be drafted from the villages in groups of five and that each member receive different technical training. At least one should become a medical corpsman, one skilled in construction, etc. Then, when the young men returned to the village they should be encouraged to return as a team, with access to low interest, long-term credit and low-priced materials.[21] What he had in mind, apparently, was the formation of small village development corporations based on skills acquired during military training.

For a time (1961–63), any lycée graduate, or graduate of a school of comparable level, could serve out the bulk of his military service as a reserve officer teacher (*yedek subay öğretmen*). When the law was changed so that only university graduates were given automatic reserve officer status, this system was ended. However, it is still true that if a lycée graduate passes a teacher's examination (*öğretmen imtihanı*), he can work off his military service as a soldier teacher (*er öğretmen*) in a primary school. To prepare himself for such an examination, the lycée graduate may take summer courses in children's literature, teaching methods, educational psychology, educational sociology, school organization, and administration.

ON-THE-JOB TRAINING

Very little of a statistical nature can be reported about on-the-job training in Turkey. But the processes at work can be defined. First, the Turkish guild structure (*esnaf*) includes a recruitment, apprenticeship, and licensing procedure which is now reinforced by law. The advantage of maintaining an *esnaf* classification rather than that of industrial labor is that the former avoids inclusion within the social welfare and security legislation and thus avoids a tax imposed on both worker and employer. Also, because of the difficulty of policing all workplaces, this body of welfare law is applicable generally only to those at which more than ten individuals are employed. Because of associated taxes, a patron will consider the addition of the eleventh worker very carefully. More likely, he will set up a different workplace if he is expanding his operations. There is thus a pressure toward industrial fragmentation built into the system which slows down the rate of mechanization and, hence, the acquisition of modern industrial skills, both technical and managerial. This process, plus the power of the guilds — which consist essentially of artisans — has constituted rigidities in the system.

The large state plants, some of which were set up originally more for the purpose of education and regional development than for internal financial profit, have become important industrial training centers. At the start, labor turnover was typically very high in many of these establishments. It was planned that way, with much of the labor force being housed in bachelor dormitories. This deliberate intrusion into traditional society was possible on this scale only through industrial enterprise concerned with generating long-run regional growth, not with short-run internal profit — and hence via state enterprise. As the labor force stabilized, skills were accumulated, a market developed, and private enterprise thus made feasible. The foremen and skilled labor in many private plants received their initial industrial training in a state enterprise. Contemporary planners recognize the importance of on-the-job training and have required foreign investors to train their own Turkish understudies, both on the technical and managerial levels. Thus, the capacity to guarantee the repatriation of capital and profits has been used as a lever to force the transfer of high-level skills.

IMPORT AND EXPORT OF HIGH-LEVEL MANPOWER

The import of high-level manpower does not seem to have been of critical significance in the formation of human capital. The influx of civilian technical assistants under United States and United Nations auspices has been helpful, though not startling. Many of these experts remained only a short time and have had a minimal effect on developing more highly skilled Turks because of their inability to communicate effectively. This is not to say that their technical findings were not of great utility. Also, private foreign business has imported some foreign managers and technicians, but there is really no way of measuring their impact. Certainly university assistance in the area of management and professional education has been of great importance. Cases in point: the Harvard Business School's help in establishing and staffing the Institute of Business Administration in Istanbul; New York University's association with the Institute of Public Administration in Ankara; University of Nebraska support for Atatürk University; Columbia University's faculty exchange system with Robert College. Foundation aid has tended to flow into either research or professional education. The Rockefeller Foundation aid to the Haccetepe Hospital in Ankara, now part of the Haccetepe Science Center, is a recent example of the latter. Perhaps the most important foreign agency for the transmission of high-level manpower has been the Joint American Military Aid Mission to Turkey, whose primary task from the start was seen to be the modernization of the Turkish military establishment, a process equated very largely with education, technical training, and changes in attitude. Furthermore, the impact of the imported military manpower was felt at all levels — general staff, officer corps, noncommissioned ranks, and privates. Evidence supporting the claim that the military has been subjected to a more rapid modernization process than the civilian population lies in the fact that eventually the military became so impatient with the relative lack of civilian enlightenment that it resolved in 1960 to intervene politically.

In the public sector other than the military, the most important impact of foreign personnel — in terms of high-level manpower development — has undoubtedly been in the administration of various of the state enterprises, specifically, the public highways, chemical industry, coal mining, the steel industry, Turkish airlines, power development, and in the planning function.

Other than the export of skilled labor to western Europe, the only other significant leakage has been via the educational route. Again, no statistics are at hand, but perhaps something on the order of 10 to 20 per cent of the youth Turkey sends abroad for study in western Europe and the United States fail to return. The charge has also been made — but largely undocumented so far as one can learn — that there are many hundreds of Turkish medical doctors practicing abroad.[22] The figures for the number of doctors practicing within Turkey (see Table 23) and the number of medical students (see Table 31) do, in fact, beg a question. The number of physicians should be going up by annual increments of 500 to 1,000. Instead, the number actually fell off between 1960 and 1962. Why? Were they simply lost to the profession by going into politics or by retiring? Or had they emigrated? One suspects that the latter reason was of considerable importance because of (1) the congestion of doctors in the Istanbul, Ankara, and Izmir regions, (2) the horror with which a professional man contemplates residence elsewhere in Turkey, and (3) the severe shortage of nurses.

Of the Turks seeking jobs in Germany, there are some statistics as to their skill level. A small sample of this group was taken in September 1963, the results of which are shown in Table 33. As can be seen, somewhat over a third of those

TABLE 33. EDUCATIONAL ACCOMPLISHMENT OF TURKISH WORKERS
IN GERMANY
(in percentages)

No schooling	2.8%
Literate (finished first 3 grades)	14.8
Finished primary school (5 years)	49.0
Institute or vocational school graduate	15.4
Middle school graduate	12.8
Lycée graduate	4.3
University or higher school graduate	0.8
Unknown	0.2

Source: Nermin Abadan, *Batĭ Almanyadakĭ Türk İşçileri ve Sorunlarĭ* (Ankara: Başkanlĭk Devlet Matbaasĭ, 1964), p. 61.

questioned had received formal education beyond primary school, which was many times the percentage for the general population (possibly 2 to 3 per cent). The same study reported that of those who went to Germany, 82.8 per cent had been gainfully employed in Turkey.[23] Their last employment in Turkey is shown in Table 34. About 85 per cent of these individuals are employed in the Federal Republic of Germany and 10 per cent in Belgium. Note that Table 35 is based on gross figures for Turks going abroad through the employment service. If one adds in those who go abroad by

TABLE 34. LAST EMPLOYMENT IN TURKEY OF TURKS
WORKING IN GERMANY
(in percentages)

Professions (medical doctor, nurse, etc.)	5.2%
Administrative personnel	7.0
Sales	4.8
Agriculture	8.8
Mining	2.6
Transport and communication	9.5
Small craftsmen	20.8
Industrial labor	25.3
Services	4.2
Unclassified	11.8

Source: Abadan, *Batı Almanyadaki Türk İşçileri ve Sorunları*, p. 71.

other channels, less the total number of returnees, possibly another 10,000 to 20,000 should be added to the 1965 year-end-total. By mid-1966 another 20,000 to 30,000 had sought European employment, and perhaps another 5,000 had returned. Therefore, the number of Turks in Europe as of mid-1966 was probably in the neighborhood of 200,000. According to a statement by the Turkish Minister of Labor in Bonn in late 1964, he anticipated that up to 300,000 Turkish workers would have found employment in western Europe before the end of the first five-year plan in 1967.

The unanswered question is what proportion of the 200,-000 Turks now employed in western Europe will return, how soon, and what will be their impact? There is some reason to

TABLE 35. TURKISH WORKERS SENT ABROAD BY THE TURKISH
EMPLOYMENT SERVICE

YEAR	MALE	FEMALE	ANNUAL TOTAL	CUMULATIVE
1961			1,636	1,636
	12,083	578		
1962	na	na	11,025	12,661
1963	27,751	2,577	30,328	42,989
1964	62,000	4,176	66,176	109,165
1965	40,347	11,179	51,526	160,691

Source: *1966 Mali Yılı Bütçe Tasarısına Ait Gerekçe* (Ankara: Government of Turkey, 1965).

believe that this group constitutes a potentially dynamic
element which has been unable to find a satisfactory place
in Turkish society as it is presently constituted. For example,
40.5 per cent of those sampled in Germany in 1963 indicated
that their place of residence was Istanbul, but only 17.4 per
cent had been born there. Comparable figures for Ankara,
7.3 and 2.2 per cent; for Izmir, 5.5 and 4.0 per cent.[24] One
should further note that some 29.2 per cent of these Turkish
expatriates reported that their permanent residence was a
village; 51.1 per cent, the cities of Istanbul, Ankara, and
Izmir; 19.8 per cent, provincial towns.[25] All of this indicates
that the *newer* city dwellers are disproportionately represented among the emigrant workers. Psychologically, these
people may have already broken with traditional society of
village and small town, and now it would appear that they
find the Turkish city society likewise inadequate. Furthermore, these persons are amassing financial resources, not
otherwise available to them in Turkey, by means of their
work in western Europe. Hence, one has here a dynamic
group in possession of financial resources. All that it lacks is
high-level skill. Turkish planners might well give close attention to the problem of exploiting this resource upon its
return to Turkey and, indeed, of taking measures to ensure
that a high percentage will return to the country.

Some thought has been given to this problem. In the first
place, worker remittances to Turkey are subject to a premium
exchange rate of about 27 per cent. The actual transfer mechanism has been made simple, inexpensive, and fast. In 1965,
approximately $70 million was sent home by Turkish workers
abroad, which was about 15.2 per cent of Turkey's export
earnings or 12.1 per cent of its import bill. The 1966 estimate
is between $90 and $100 million, but it could conceivably be
$130 million. The proportion saved and banked abroad is
not known, but it may be as high as $100 million.[26]

The Turkish government has also established a system of importation with waiver of the usual restrictions on imports by Turkish nationals. Among the qualifications is that a person must have spent at least two years' service or training abroad. Another is that in order to bring in a car under the system, a person must have had a monthly remuneration of not less than $150, and a savings account in the amount of more than $800 (raised from $600 previously). Moreover, automobiles to be imported under the waiver system must not be more than five years old.[27] Only factory and office workers are eligible for the foreign exchange and import waiver premiums. Professional people, such as medical doctors, are barred.

More specifically designed to encourage the workers to return is a mortgage loan scheme, an investment scheme, and an employment scheme. Turkish laborers who obtain jobs abroad through the Turkish Employment Bureau can open housing credit accounts in the Türkiye Emlak Kredi Bankasï. The savings of these workers deposited with the Housing Credit Fund earn 6.5 per cent annual interest. After the emigrant worker has deposited a minimum of TL 5,000 ($555) in the fund (but not more than TL 10,000, or $1,111), he is eligible for a loan equal to his deposit, plus up to four times his deposit, or TL 40,000 ($4,444). Terms are 20 years at 2 per cent. The apartment or house he decides upon must be of modest proportions — no more than 70 square meters of floor space — and he, himself, must have returned to Turkey to implement the loan. The attraction of these loans is their relatively low interest rate.

The other credit arrangement open to Turkish workers who remit their funds is a small business credit and loan setup similar to the housing credits, but on less generous terms. This system makes possible small investment credits against savings in foreign exchange by workers employed abroad who wish to return and establish small businesses in Turkey. The investment credit is for three to five times the workers' savings account, but is not to exceed TL 75,000 ($8,355). The loans are for five years at 7 per cent, with a one-year grace period. Unfortunately, "these credit arrangements, the housing and the small business loans, have been largely ineffective in attracting remittances. Figures on the housing account are not available, but it is known that the amount put into the small business loan plan as of September 1965 was a paltry TL 212,765 ($19,500 at the premium rate). It is estimated that only one per cent of the workers have availed themselves of this mechanism." [28]

A recently-conceived mechanism to put workers' remittances to constructive use is a government decision to aid them in setting up joint stock companies for investing in Turkish industries. The aim is to provide profits and employment to the workers on their return from abroad, and the state has offered to take a 25 per cent equity position in these undertakings. A pilot project company has been started by 100 Turkish workers in Cologne under the name of TURK-SAN, Industrial and Commercial Corporation of Turkey. The Turkish government has also instituted a program designed to encourage rural workers to go abroad. Priority of employment opportunities is to be given to those villagers who form cooperatives of between 100 to 200 workers. The plan calls for each villager sent abroad to transfer TL 350 to 400 monthly ($39–44) out of his earnings. Thus at the end of a year it will be possible for these cooperatives to establish joint stock companies in their villages with a capital of TL 500,000 to 1,000,000 ($55,555–$111,111). The purpose of the companies is to make investments in agriculture, transportation, and industry. Each member of the cooperative will be authorized to import capital goods such as mechanical ploughs, tractors, and machinery, up to a value of TL 10,000

($1,111), under the provisions of the legislation on imports, without allocation of foreign exchange.[29]

Considerable interest is reported among Turkish workers abroad in another scheme whereby the foreign exchange sent home by them would be accumulated in a special fund for the purpose of investing in domestic industry. Although not yet implemented, it is proposed that the stock of such enterprises would be owned by the workers making contributions. Upon returning home, they would be given preferential right in securing jobs in these companies. In short, it would be a form of Emigrants' Savings Development Bank with hiring privileges for the stockholders.[30]

A feedback has apparently set in, for wherever the author traveled in Turkey during the summer of 1965 he found many villages and townsmen contemplating a period of work in Germany. In one village in which a Village Development Association had been organized, 160 men had signed up to go to Europe in order to secure capital for village projects. Each had pledged to repatriate TL 150 per month for this purpose. Also, very much a part of the Anatolian scene in August 1965 were many hundreds of men back in their home communities for a month-long vacation from their European jobs.

The main flows of high-level manpower are generated by the Turkish educational system (public and private), foreign educational experience, a variety of adult vocational schools and courses, the military training programs, and on-the-job training with some assistance from imported high-level manpower. In addition, there are some 200,000 Turkish workers presently employed in western Europe, but it is much too early to assess their contribution to the high-level skill pool within Turkey.

CHART IX. MANPOWER REQUIREMENTS: 1977, BY TYPE
OF OCCUPATION AND SOURCE AND SUPPLY

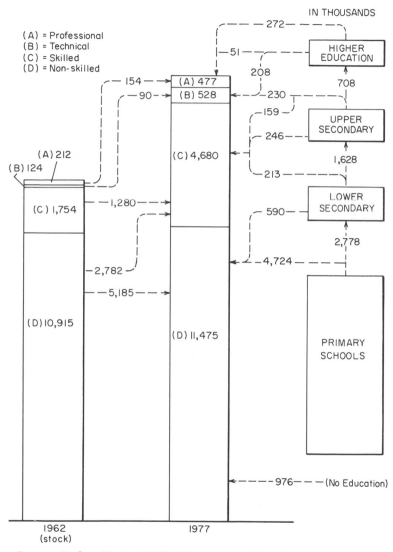

Source: *Turkey* (Paris: OECD Education and Development Country Reports, Mediterranean Regional Project, 1965), p. 54.

It is quite clear that the educational system must be the major source of supply, but it is equally clear that the capacity of the present system is far short of satisfying the need either now or in the foreseeable future. Chart IX diagrams the problem. Dotted lines indicate the added capacity needed by 1977. Because the educational system is unlikely to generate this augmented flow, the full resources of the military establishment, foreign educational institutions, on-the-job training in industry, and imported skills offered by both Turks and non-Turks will be required. Education — even basic education — need not take place within a "school."

The difficulty of recruiting faculty for institutions of higher learning in the smaller centers of Anatolia remains. An interesting recent suggestion by the Minister of Education: as a condition for appointment as assistant or associate professor, two years of teaching in an institution outside of Istanbul, Ankara, and Izmir.[15]

VII

THE PROCESS OF ALLOCATION

In any traditional society that is only very incompletely on a cash basis and for which the concept of a national market is very new, potential differences in income do not adequately explain the choice of occupation. Compensation is more likely to be defined in social-psychological rewards. For the ordinary Anatolian villager, who is still a member of traditional society, the thought of leaving the land would be entirely alien. For him, there simply is no choice.

Several events can bring about a change in this attitude: (1) inability of a parent to cope with a changing social environment, (2) compulsory secular education of a post-Newtonian variety, (3) military training away from home in a technologically and achievement-oriented army, (4) geographic and occupational mobility forced by economic pressures (or by social pressures, as in the case of rural Shiite groups). The initial reaction of a village youth who is breaking with traditional society may be to set up a household for himself and his wife physically apart from that of his father before the death of the latter. The desire for privacy may compel him to build a house separated from the village, which is typically a tight cluster of extended family households. If this sets off a family quarrel, he may be forced to seek work elsewhere than on his father's land, hence an exploratory move to the city where some of the skills acquired while in the army may be useful. Once he sees his way to making a living in this new environment, a permanent move may be made. The point is that employment possibilities in the city are very frequently only a secondary reason for the change. Any move motivated by purely economic reasons (such as the temporary urban employment of younger sons of a land-hungry family) is less likely for a variety of factors, including (1) crop subsidies, (2) land distribution to the landless or near landless village families, and (3) virtual tax exemption of agricultural wealth and income.

There is a demonstrable tendency for both groups — the psychologically and economically motivated — to gravitate very quickly toward Istanbul, Ankara, Adana, and Izmir, and, to a somewhat lesser extent, Kayseri, Eskişehir, Gaziantep, and Bursa. (For example, see Chart X, which is based on a study of the flow of workers out of the eastern provinces.) The smaller provincial centers provide neither the anonymity (hence, security) nor the job opportunity to attract either group. Nor do they provide the educational and health facilities frequently associated with these motives. Typically, the new urban dweller starts with menial labor or semi-skilled construction work. If he has been a noncommissioned officer, he may quickly find himself a role as straw boss or foreman. Wage differentials are substantial as between foreman and common laborer, being on the order of 3 or 2 to 1 (see Table 36). It is also significant that private management is more highly paid than the managers of public enterprise in relationship to common labor, as well as in absolute terms. This differential is perhaps in part a function of the greater psychic income (via prestige) perceived by a public functionary.

Despite the wage differential between foreman and laborer, for many Turks the added responsibility that a foreman carries does not seem to be worth the price. In general, the whole range of "middle-skilled" or "subprofessional" per-

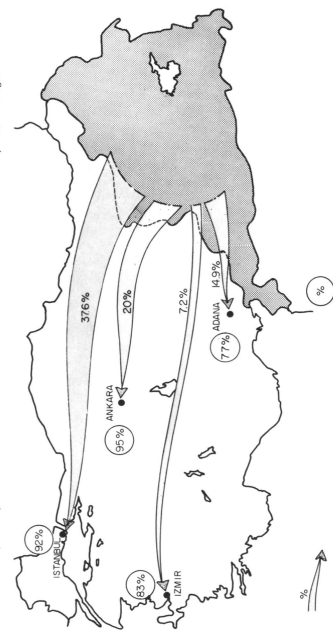

CHART X. SETTLEMENT OF MIGRANTS FROM THE EASTERN PROVINCES IN ISTANBUL, ANKARA, IZMIR AND SEYHAN (ADANA) PROVINCES AND THE DEGREE OF URBAN SETTLEMENT IN EACH CASE, PRIOR TO 1960

Arrows indicate percentage of migrants going to the four provinces indicated.

Circles indicate percentage of migrants going to each province who settle in cities with a population of over 10,000.

TABLE 36. MONTHLY WAGE AND SALARY RATES, 1962

CLASS OF EMPLOYEE	RANGE	MEDIAN	RATIO TO COMMON LABOR
In a Typical State Plant			
General manager	2363–2700 TL	2531	6.6/1
Department superintendent	1485–2362	1924	5.0/1
Senior engineer	1080–2363	1221	3.2/1
Junior engineer	945–2363	1654	4.3/1
Office help (incl. accountants, clerks)	608–1688	1148	2.9/1
Foreman	600–948	774	2.0/1
Mechanics	516–732	624	1.6/1
Common labor	264–504	384	1.0/1
In Private Metal Working Shops		(mean)	
General managers	2060–6050	4640	10.3/1
Engineers	900–8500	3920	8.7/1
Accountants	1000–4000	2260	5.2/1
General foreman	1220–4100	2130	4.7/1
Technicians	1000–2500	1530	3.4/1
Foreman	610–2500	1410	3.1/1
Office help, unspecified	350–5450	1280	2.9/1
Skilled workers	170–2500	975	2.2/1
Semi-skilled workers	120–980	535	1.2/1
Unskilled workers	230–700	450	1.0/1
Apprentices	50–500	240	.5/1

Source: *Investment Guide to Turkey* (Ankara: Union of Chambers of Commerce, Industry and Commodity Exchanges of Turkey, 1964), p. 60.

sonnel — foreman, clerk, nurse, technician — are probably grossly underpaid in terms of the marginal value to society of these jobs. But more important than that, traditional society really had no comparable roles other than that of the noncommissioned officer in the army and his counterpart in the government hierarchy. There was the artisan, but typically his management role was very limited. One was either a member of the rural or urban elite, or of the rural or urban mass. Nor did the traditional elite know how to use middle management effectively. It dared not delegate authority; that would have undermined its own prestige and hence, power, for this was largely an ascriptive society, not an achievement-oriented one. Middle management — whether nurse or foreman — was equally reluctant to accept authority, for that would have set up obligations or responsibilities for which their social origins ill prepared them. To accept responsibilities introduces an element of risk and, in a near subsistence situation, risk can be costly.

Based on a 1954–55 survey, a prestige ranking of occupations among a sample of lycée students was recorded (see Table 37). The author of this study concluded:

In general, occupations requiring high degree of skill, long training, and mental rather than physical effort are to be found toward the top of the list, particularly if they involve governmental or public service, and to a lesser extent if they are well paid. Work that is physical, particularly if it is low income, is characteristic of the occupations toward the bottom of the list. Linked to these qualities, the higher prestige occupations tend to be the kind that Turkey shares with the Western nations, the lesser respected ones those that continue traditional Middle Eastern culture.

In writing of a country where quantitative social description is far less abundant than we would like, the question that we must attempt, at least, to answer is: Are the findings for this sample generalizable to any population beyond itself?

The answer must be a cautious "no." A sample of 310 cases is small in relation to any national population segment and it was not randomly drawn.[1]

But by the same token, it would indeed be unusual if the subject group for this study were unique. Indeed, other bits and pieces of evidence would generally support this ranking. The author points out that the more "cosmopolitan" an individual is, the lower he is inclined to rank the religious leader and professional soldier, and the higher he ranks professional and business occupations.[2]

Another relevant study was that made by Kazamias in 1964, who found that among lycée students questioned, the "free professions" were most respected. Students were given a list of eleven occupational categories and were asked to rank them according to the prestige and respect which, in

TABLE 37. SIXTY-THREE TURKISH OCCUPATIONS RANKED FROM HIGHEST
TO LOWEST IN PRESTIGE
(N = 310)

Doktor (physician) 94.36
Üniversite profesörü (univ.
    prof.) 93.26
Mebus (member of parliament) 92.91
Vali (chief provincial
    administrator) 92.24
Albay (colonel) 92.08
Vekil (cabinet minister) 91.80
Mühendis (engineer) 90.70
Hakim (judge) 90.32
Avukat (lawyer) 88.58
Fen adamı (scientist) 86.99
Fabrikatör (manufacturer) . . . 83.46
Kaymakam (chief county
    administrator) 82.24
Lise öğretmeni (high school
    teacher) 81.80
Banka müdürü (bank director) 81.68
Eczaci (druggist) 81.00
Müfettiş (official inspector) . . . 80.52
Muharrir (professional writer) 78.80
Dişci (dentist) 78.06
Teğmen (lieutenant) 77.34
Politikacı (politician) 71.70
Veteriner (veterinary) 70.33
Köy öğretmeni (village school
    teacher) 70.02
Çiftlik sahibi (agricultural
    landlord) 69.10
Gazeteci (journalist) 68.72
Konser piyanisti (concert
    pianist) 67.18
Ressam (artist, painter) 67.18
Sekreter (secretary) 65.03
Memur (government official) . 64.58
Büyük dükkânci (retailer,
    large store) 61.92
Muhasîp (accountant) 60.78
Er (soldier, private) 59.95

Hoca (religious teacher) 59.31
Imam (leader of public
    worship) 56.16
Teatro artisti (dramatic actor) 55.28
Hafız (religious reciter) 54.60
Köy muhtarı (village
    headman) 53.31
Terzi (tailor) 53.13
Bakkal (grocer) 52.51
Saatcı (watch repairman) 52.20
Köylü çiftçi (village farmer,
    peasant) 52.05
Gemici (sailor) 51.05
Otomobil tamircisi (auto
    repairman) 50.24
Marangoz (carpenter) 48.69
Kunduracı (shoemaker) 44.77
Berber (barber) 44.00
Küçük dükkânci (shopkeeper) 42.13
Şoför (professional driver,
    truck/car) 40.92
Kasap (butcher) 39.42
Bakırcı (coppersmith) 38.01
Bina boyacısı (housepainter) . . 36.82
Bahçevan (gardener) 36.21
Balıkçı (fisherman) 35.12
Kebapçı (small short-order
    rest. prop.) 33.33
Garson (waiter) 28.28
Sokak satıcısı (street vendor) . 24.85
Çoban (shepherd) 22.26
Eskürbacı (used clothing
    dealer) 21.61
Meyhaneci (tavern keeper) . . . 20.76
Deveci (camel driver) 20.57
Kapıcı (doorkeeper) 19.41
Hizmetçi (servant) 17.24
Hammal (porter) 16.28
Dilenci (beggar) 14.64

Source: Based on survey of 310 lycée students in Ankara, İçel, İzmir and
Kayseri, 1955. See George Helling, "Changing Attitudes Toward Occupational Status and Prestige in Turkey" (Omaha: University of Omaha, un-
dated but probably 1958, mimeographed).

Table 38. Percentage of Lycée Students Ranking Each Occupation
as Being Highest in Public Esteem

	All Students	Boys
Free profession	43%	47%
Diplomat	27	24
Education	6.6	7
Business man ("big")	6	7
Military officer	5	7
Religion	2	3
National government official	2	2
Farm owner	1	less than 1
Business executive or official	1	less than 1
Skilled labor	0	0
In the "free profession" category		
Scientist	31%	32%
Engineer	29	33
Medical doctor	22	19.5
Lawyer	7	7
Pharmacist	3	2.4
Religious leader	2	2.5
Journalist	1.8	2
Dentist	1	1
In the government category (i.e., local and national)		
Diplomat	33%	29
Deputy in the National Assembly	31	35
Provincial governor (vali)	14	17.5
Judge	7	7
Military officer	3	3.7
Governor of a sub-province (kaymakam)	2.3	3.5
National government official	1.0	1.1
Regional director (müdur)	1.0	1.3
Noncommissioned officer	.3	less than 1
Village headman (muhtar)	.3	less than 1
District director (nahiye müdürü)	.1	0

Source: Kazamias, "Education and the Quest for Modernity in Turkey,"
pp. 283–84.

their opinion, the people of Turkey accorded them. Table 38
shows how the students ranked as number one the various
occupational clusters.

Kazamias reports further,

Regarding occupations classified under "education," the majority of
the students (58 percent), and of both the boys and the girls (57 and
67 percent respectively) ranked "university professor" highest in pres-

tige. The occupation which received the next highest number of "one" votes by all the students and by the boys was "national education director" (*milli eğitim müdürü*); "elementary school teacher" came third for the group as a whole (9 per cent) as well as for the boys (10 percent); and *"lise* teacher" quite surprisingly was fourth (6 percent of all the students).[3]

One suspects that because the prestige item may be of relatively greater importance than in the more achievement-oriented societies of the industrial West, salary and wage differentials must be even greater if any departure from the traditional pattern is to be effected.

Among lycée students, Professor Kazamias found that 82 per cent of the students from urban areas and only 18 per cent of those from rural areas reported that their parents had a lycée diploma. He also found that 75 per cent of the students' parents were from the city or town in which their lycée was located. Therefore, the pressure of parental achievement and geographical proximity to a lycée would appear important in determining the flow of students into lycées. For a village youth to enter a lycée represents a much greater break with family tradition, and implies greater geographical mobility. Therefore, one might expect a higher incidence of truly creative personalities among lycée students of village origin. Unfortunately, Kazamias did not correlate expectations with origin. It is of significance to note, however, that of all of the students questioned, he found 67.4 per cent were attending a lycée rather than a vocational school in order to continue education at the university level, 13.1 per cent to get a broad education.

Nonetheless, wage differentials as among occupations and regions likewise set up allocational pressures. The differentials shown in Table 39 are undoubtedly a function of the more adequate supply of labor for the more traditional occupations, i.e., farm labor, mining, logging, fishing, personal services. The top-level or white-collar jobs show an inade-

TABLE 39. AVERAGE DAILY WAGES, 1962

Mining (including coal)	12.02 TL	Paper	17.35
Farm labor	12.50	Leather products	17.85
Logging	12.80	Transport equipment	18.13
Quarrying	12.87	Electrical equipment	18.64
Coal mining	13.54	Metal goods	19.14–19.72
Personal services	13.85	Chemicals	19.59
Fishing	14.14	Machinery	20.88
Construction	16.94	Petroleum	22.86
Public water and health		Publishing and	
services	17.00	printing	25.95
Entertainment	18.10	Petroleum products	34.62
Industry	18.43	Communications	18.90
Tobacco products	11.59	Warehousing	19.95
Food products	13.76	Transportation	19.47
Textiles	14.55	Electrical and gas	
Earth products	15.15	utilities	19.58
Furniture	15.24	Wholesale and retail	24.75
Other	15.66	Banking	25.90
Rubber products	15.73	Insurance	26.98
Beverages	16.04		
Clothing	16.76	All	16.48

Source: İstatistik, 1960–62, pp. 349–51.

quate supply, the wage ratio being over 2 to 1 as between those in insurance and farm labor. The reason the difference is not greater is the relative surfeit of underemployed lycée and college graduates, which is an indication of a mismatching between educational flows and developmental manpower needs.

A narrowing of the gap between high- and low-level employees within the bureaucracy has been noted. "While in 1939 the highest ranking bureaucrat earned 12 times as much as the lowest ranking did, by 1961 he earned only 6.4 times as much." [4] The question is "why?" One can postulate several answers, such as growing official interest in social welfare, the increased skill level of the lowest paid government employee as compared to those on the highest level, or the increase in job competition at the higher levels. In the absence of solid evidence one way or the other, one suspects that the latter explanation bears the larger part of the responsibility. Interest in social welfare has simply not gone that far, nor have the skills required by the lowest paid job increased all that much. The hypothesis advanced here is supported by the finding that "people in the bureaucracy with a higher education are paid more for the same work and have a monopoly on promotion to the top positions." [5] This last implies that the competition is greater for positions requiring a higher education than for a lesser education — further evidence of a mismatching in the output of the educational system.

Another recent study indicates that Turks with only an elementary or secondary education are more security conscious than their compatriots who have at least some university education in the sense of preferring higher job security at the sacrifice of income.[6] An earlier study of *bureaucrats*, however, indicated the reverse, which may mean that the more security conscious tend to seek employment in the government,[7] although more recent data would indicate no differential between university-educated bureaucrats and other university-educated Turks in this respect.[8] In any event, there is no reason to believe that this difference has increased within recent years and, hence, cannot be advanced as a reason for the narrowing income gap between top- and bottom-level public servants.

The regional wage differentials (see Chart XI) may well have shrunk since 1957, at the time these calculations were made. Nonetheless, they probably pull in the same direction, not necessarily because of labor shortages, but more because of cost-of-living differentials and political pressures. One bit of relevant recent evidence is the regional variation in per capita annual farm income (see Table 40).

One student of industrial entrepreneurship in Turkey has come up with the conclusion that the single most important

TABLE 40. REGIONAL VARIATION IN PER CAPITA AGRICULTURAL INCOME

AREA	TURKISH LIRA
Thrace, Marmara, Aegean	1864
Black Sea Coast	1179
Mediterranean Coast	2003
Western Anatolia	1683
Central Anatolia	2246
South Eastern Anatolia	2305
Eastern Anatolia	1258
National Average	1759

Source: Namïk Zeki Aral, "Zirâi Coğrafyamïz," *Türkiye İktisat Gazetesi,* September 9, 1965, pp. 1–8.

group from which Turkish industrialists are recruited are traders. Larger farmers and craftsmen ranked second as a source of recruitment, each being of roughly equal importance. Virtually all of the farmers had moved into industries processing agricultural products, which was not true for the traders. Craftsmen tended to become industrialists simply by expanding their operations. "Second generation industrialists, traders, farmers and former craftsmen tend to own large industrial enterprises in that order." [9]

A more recent survey of 138 private firms in Turkey's six major cities led to the finding that 53 per cent of the industrialists and businessmen questioned had fathers in industry or business and 48 per cent of their wives' fathers had a similar background. Of these enterprises, 52 per cent were owned entirely by a family and only 24 per cent had no family relationship among shareholders, all of which leads to the conclusion that "there is still a somewhat distinct social group for most of the entrepreneurs." [10] Sixty-nine per cent of these entrepreneurs also functioned as shareholder and manager. Their educational background was: 38 per cent university graduates, 31 per cent lycée graduates, 11 per cent elementary school graduates, 1.4 per cent without any formal schooling. Eighty-three per cent were of Turkish ethnic origin, 9 per cent Jewish, and 7 per cent Greek. "When one takes into consideration the fact that the percentage in the general population is 0.2 per cent Jewish and 0.35 per cent Greek, the relative importance of these two ethnic groups in industry can be easily observed." "Yet," the author concludes, "it is a fair conclusion that their relative importance is decreasing." [11]

Another flow that has been plotted is in the bureaucracy, where kinship seems to count very heavily. A 1964 survey of high-level Turkish bureaucrats indicated that roughly half had had career public servants as fathers. About one-third reported grandfathers with government service under the Sultan.[12] The same survey turned up data showing a similar continuity among middle-level bureaucrats. In other words, considerable family continuity in respect to bureaucratic recruitment is demonstrated, particularly when one bears in mind the expansion of the bureaucratic work force under the Republic. Even so, as already noted, the salaries of bureaucrats rose at a much slower rate relative to other occupations in Turkish society, the former's buying power being cut approximately in half between 1939 and 1961. "Job openings in the bureaucracy have also been less numerous than in other sections of the economy over the past few years," the 1955–1960 increase in the number of high-level administrative and executive personnel in the government being only 4,654. "During this same period, the private sector hired 48,595 additional high-level administrators." The 1960 totals for the government and private sectors were 17,194 and 67,415, respectively.[13] It is not surprising, therefore, that the tendency for graduates of the Political Science Faculty of the University of Ankara to leave government service is increasing, although well over half still enter the public sector.[14]

It would appear that the traditional processes controlling the allocation of high-level manpower are beginning to break

CHART XI. AVERAGE DAILY WAGE FOR WORKPLACES COVERED BY
SOCIAL WELFARE LAWS FOR 22 PROVINCES, 1957

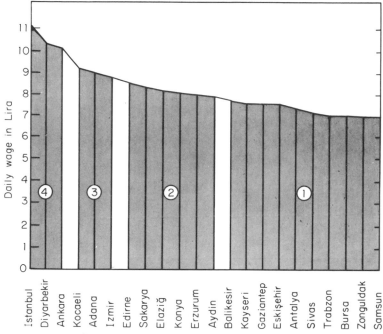

Source: *Türkiye İktisat Gazetesi*, April 9, 1959, p. 4.

down. Although we lack an historical series of occupational
preference studies, it seems highly unlikely that the ranking
reported in either Table 37 or 38 would have been valid for,
say, 1940. The scientist, the engineer, and the medical doctor
are being taken as principal models by lycée students. Also
there is some measurable evidence indicating a break in the
father-son occupational sequence in both agriculture and
government administration. The Frey study of the political
elite demonstrates a growing regional identity, as opposed
to the more nationally-oriented elite of the 1920–1940 era.
The Roos study of the bureaucratic elite indicates a similar
growth of regionalism. And, as can be seen from Chart XI

and Table 40, despite a growing mobility of the population, significant regional differences in income levels have not been ironed out. It is apparent that large numbers of people do not find the trade off between added income and moving to be sufficiently attractive to lure them from their traditional homes. Another explanation, already advanced, is that the more talented and motivated individuals move toward higher income areas leaving behind them their less well endowed compatriots. Hence, the income differentials persist. The net result would seem to be the congregation in the large urban centers of the western part of the country of the modernists and transitionalists and a stiffening of the more traditional elements remaining behind in the villages and small towns, particularly in the eastern and central provinces. This tendency, plus the growing regionalism of the political elite, may well bring about a restructuring of the political parties — western modernists pitted against central and eastern traditionalists, the latter being aided and abetted by opportunist politicians. The danger is that in the rush to create the high-level skills required by Turkey's forced draft development the country will be torn apart.

VIII

POLICY IMPLICATIONS
AND CONCLUSIONS

Assuming that expansion of the GNP implies a comparable expansion of high-level manpower, and that the planners achieve their 7 per cent–per annum growth rate, how many persons embodying high-level skills need be made available each year? Going back to Table 15 we can derive a 1960 H/L ratio (i.e., high-level manpower/total labor force) of 199/12760, or roughly 1/64 (i.e., 1.6 per cent). From Table 20, which relates to industry and services only, the ratio is 142/12993, or 1.1 per cent, for 1962. Any projection of these proportionalities into the future is based on the assumptions that (1) the 1960 or 1962 ratio was adequate to sustain the 7 per cent growth rate, (2) that the efficiency of high-level manpower will neither increase nor decrease, (3) that the labor force as a percentage of total population will not shift significantly.

The first assumption is open to debate. The second is open to even more serious question. The *efficiency* of high-level manpower is a function of (1) the degree to which the supply of specific skills are matched with those needed; (2) the extent to which associated jobs requiring lesser skills (e.g., subprofessional, middle management) are performed by other than high-level manpower; (3) the extent to which those receiving high-level skills possess creative personalities (i.e., those with high need achievement), intelligence, and physical energy (including an adequately long life expectancy to warrant the initial investment in them). Surely, several if not all of these factors will shift in value.

The third assumption — the stable labor force percentage — is likewise unjustified in the face of the massive shift off the land and into the city, from the farm to the industrial labor market. Among other things, the percentage of gainfully employable women in urban households may be, for purposes of tabulating the size of the labor force, substantially less than for rural society. Work in the family fields is "labor"; work in household chores is not!

If Turkish plans are examined from these points of view, they fail on several counts. By 1967, a labor force of 14.9 million is expected; by 1977, 19.2 million. If the 1/64 ratio held, some 238,000 high-level personnel would be needed by 1967, and 307,000 by 1977. In fact, from Table 20 we see that 220,000 of such persons are planned by 1967, 421,000 by 1977 in industry and services alone (these totals are obtained by adding the figures in the first two lines of Table 20). Apparently a somewhat higher H/L ratio is believed optimum in the long run by the planners, something in the neighborhood of 1/46 for industry and services (see Table 41).

An increase in the H/L ratio of this magnitude, from 1/87 to 1/46, requires a net annual inflow of high-level personnel of about 20,000, which means a gross inflow of perhaps 22,000 in order to make some allowance for the outflow rate (e.g., retirement, death, and emigration). From what source do the entrants come? The flow of students out of the relevant institutions apparently does not fulfill the need (see Table 42). By 1977, the planners seem to assume that their HLM needs will be met; there is no indication of a contrary assumption. But there is no ready explanation for the rather violent shift in the relationship between the needed annual

TABLE 41. PROJECTED HIGH-LEVEL MANPOWER NEEDS IN INDUSTRY AND SERVICES

	1962	1963	1964	1965	1966	1967	1972	1977
HLM supply	146,000	156,000	164,000	179,000	206,000	220,000	331,000	421,000
HLM flow/yr.	—	10,000	20,000	15,000	21,000	20,000	22,000	18,000
Labor force*	12.7m.	13.1m.	13.5m.	13.9m.	14.4m.	14.9m.	16.9m.	19.2m.
H/L ratio	1/87	1/84	1/82	1/78	1/72	1/68	1/51	1/46

Source: Calculated from Tables 17 and 20.
* In millions.

TABLE 42. INFLOW OF HIGH-LEVEL PERSONNEL

	1963	1964	1965	1966	1967	1972	1977
1. Annual need, net[a]	10,000	20,000	15,000	21,000	20,000	22,000	18,000
2. Annual need, gross[b]	11,000	22,000	16,000	23,000	22,000	24,000	20,000
3. Students in adv. tech. and general educ. inst.[c]	63,000	68,000	72,000	77,000	88,000	180,000	227,000
4. Ratio (line 2:3)	17%	32%	22%	30%	25%	13%	9%
5. Realistic flow, 10% of line 3[d]	6,300	6,800	7,200	7,700	8,800	18,000	23,000
6. Net annual shortage (2–5)	−4,700	−15,200	−8,800	−15,300	−13,200	−6,000	+3,000
7. Cumulative shortage	−4,700	−19,900	−28,700	−44,000	−53,200	−59,200	−56,200

[a] From Table 41, projected by planners.
[b] Line 1 + 10%
[c] From Table 24, projected by planners.
[d] Might improve in future.

inflow of high-level manpower personnel and the number of students enrolled in institutions capable of turning out such manpower (32 per cent to 9 per cent).

In fact, not more than 10 per cent of those enrolled in high-level educational institutions can be expected to move into the labor force in any one year (1960 ratio for Ankara University, diplomas awarded to number of students, 1,373/17,881; for the University of Istanbul, 741/1,279; for Istanbul Technical University, 537/2,682; for all higher schools other than universities 6,025/65,297).[1] A more realistic flow into the high-level manpower pool from the educational system (i.e., 10 per cent of those registered in high-level institutions) generates a net deficit in the development of new high-level manpower on the order of between 4,700 and 15,300, leveling off finally along about 1975 to an equilibrium figure (see Table 42). Apparently, the planners anticipate no improvement in the enrollment-diploma ratio. Otherwise, anticipated 1977 enrollment need not be so high.

If the present level of subprofessional and middle management personnel is inadequate to permit full employment of high-level personnel, the latter's numbers will have to be increased even more rapidly. Yet, in Table 24 it will be noted that 1972 and 1977 index numbers for students in technical and vocational schools at lycée level do not increase significantly in relation to advanced technical and general advanced education. Indeed, in the case of the technical lycées and advanced technical education, the ratio between the two drops: 280/270 (1: 96) in 1967, 613/640 (1:105) in 1972, and 840/840 (1:1) in 1977. And the index number for regular lycée students slips rather badly in respect to those for higher level students (from 112:110 in 1967 to 195:227 in 1972 to 237:280 in 1977). This suggests that the professional/subprofessional and management/middle management ratios will deteriorate, meaning even less efficient use of high-level manpower in years to come. If this is true, then the inflow into the high-level manpower pool will have to be even greater than that indicated in Table 42, which means greater shortages until the inflow can be stepped up.

Perhaps more serious than these considerations may be the complete absence of any real effort to channel the more dynamic elements of the population towards the acquisition of high-level manpower skills. A large percentage of the present lycée and university students are not modernists; they represent a highly conservative urban element who pursue the time-honored ways. They clog the higher institutions of learning while those with high need achievement in the population find themselves blocked in their upward mobility by an inadequate public secondary school system and inadequate economic opportunity. One problem has been that many in this group are of an age normally considered well beyond school age, which suggests the inadequacy of our age-grade associations. An urban-based system of middle schools and lycées for adults (i.e., 18 or older) may be appropriate. Most of those selected for admission would have to be supported by the government, which support would have to include family maintenance as well. A special effort might be made to get those workers returning from Europe into this educational flow, as well as the new urban dwellers and army returnees, particularly the noncommissioned officers.

There remains within the existing educational process a number of rather serious deficiencies. At the primary level, one may be justifiably concerned about the curriculum content. A recent comparison published in the Turkish press is shown in Table 43. As already noted, the Ministry of Education is committed to introducing a "progressive" educational system in all of the primary schools by 1967. But no plans have been made to modernize the curricula in either

TABLE 43. CLASS HOURS IN PRIMARY SCHOOL
(five-year totals)

	TURKEY	YUGOSLAVIA	GREECE	SWITZERLAND
Total class hours	2,945	3,295	4,180	4,185
Hours in mathematics	476	897	583	998
Hours in science	130	662	408	407

Source: Dr. Cemal Yïldïrïm of the Middle East Technical University, in *Cumhuriyet*, January 2, 1965.

the middle schools or lycées, which are severely criticized by many of Turkey's top educators and others as not being optimum in producing the highly-motivated, creative, problemsolving oriented individuals Turkish development requires.[2] As one measure of this inadequacy, a recent study by experts from the Organization of European Economic Cooperation and Development (OECD) confirms that more than 15,000 primary schools (out of roughly 30,000) and 300 secondary schools (out of about 1,020) have no science teaching equipment whatsoever.[3] In other schools, where some equipment was available, either its use was restrained by the lack of foreign exchange with which to purchase replacements or it went totally unused by both students and teachers, reposing "in glass cases like museum pieces."[4]

The result of the OECD report was the formation of a joint committee of Turkish educational and technical experts and representatives of the OECD Scientific Affairs Directorate. It recommended curriculum reform in the natural sciences and initiated the establishment in Ankara of the Center for the Production of Science Teaching Instruments with a staff of 109 designers, technicians, and administrative personnel. Partially financed by the OECD, the Center's purpose is to make Turkey self-sufficient in educational scientific equipment.

Despite enormous effort, the teaching of foreign languages at the middle school and lycée levels is inadequate. In recognition of this fact, the Turkish government requested English language teachers from the Peace Corps. Robert College, the American Girls' College in Istanbul, the middle schools and lycées operated by the United Church Board for World Ministries, and the Middle East Technical University have — and are — making important contributions in this area. In addition there are German, French, and British-supported schools, plus a number of private Turkish lycées which have appeared in recent years, the so-called *"kolej,"* which teach in a foreign language. The alternative is a massive translation program. Although the Turkish government has, for the past thirty years, maintained a program of translating the world's classics into modern Turkish, it is virtually impossible to develop high-level skills on a Turkish language base only. The flow of relevant literature is simply too great.

There has been a further linguistic problem in that rapid social and technological change, based primarily on externally-generated innovation, means a large influx of foreign words and phrases into the language. So rapid is this process that unless some authority seizes the initiative to effect some degree of uniformity in spellings and definitions assigned to the ingested foreign words, utter chaos can develop very quickly. Further complicating the Turkish problem was the shift in 1928 from the Arabic script to a wholly phonetic Latin alphabet, one motive being the greater ease with which literacy might be attained. Associated with this change in the writing system was an effort to purify the language by ridding it of Persian and Arabic words and grammatical construction and substituting "pure Turkish," often resurrected from very ancient sources largely unknown to contemporary Turks. The result was that the younger generation found it difficult to communicate with the older. The Turkish government has recently published an official dictionary which somewhat helps to resolve both of these problems and of course the sheer passage of time relieves the problem. Nonetheless, these processes add to the difficulty of achieving and exercising high-level skills on a purely Turkish-language base. The acquisition of a Western language is therefore an enormous advantage.

The universities are generally poorly structured. First, there seems to be little dovetailing of the flow of students and the skills required by the society, except in the case of the Middle East Technical University, Atatürk University, and the Haccetepe Science Center.[5] Second, the percentage of university students graduating each year is very low, probably on the order of 10 per cent. Third, a large percentage of the faculty is on a part-time basis and members are present at their respective institutions only for lectures. Fourth, the enormous prestige of a university degree makes it psychologically compelling for many to go into higher education who might much better join the middle management or subprofessional groups. These criticisms are made by the Turkish educational leaders themselves.[6] The problem is of a political nature. Is the concept of complete university autonomy in such areas as admission policy and the flow of students into subject area really appropriate in the Turkish case?

For the time being, the inadequacies of the formal educational system must be balanced by (1) on-the-job training, (2) military training, (3) foreign education and training. In this regard, several policies suggest themselves. In order to stimulate more on-the-job training by business, the government might offer matching funds to private firms for such purposes. In some instances, outsiders (i.e., those not employed by the firm or not expected to be so employed) might be admitted to these privately-run courses. The lack of any apparent coordination between the military training programs and the general educational plans is a serious defect. Military training should be so geared that trainees, upon completion of stipulated courses, could enter the civilian educational hierarchy at defined levels. The army should be encouraged to develop skills specifically needed by the civilian economy. Also appealing is the idea suggested earlier that the army might draft men in groups of five or so from a given village, give each group member a useful skill, and encourage the group to return to the village as a unit. Perhaps low-interest financing and low-priced supplies might be adequate inducement for the creation of such village development corporations. It might be appropriate to enlarge the noncommissioned and commissioned officer corps, and to include in its training the type of knowledge and/or experience that will help in the transition to civilian middle management and top management levels. A speedup in the turnover in the two corps might also prove worth while. Perhaps at the end of their military tour, officers and noncoms might be sent to civilian schools of administration established specifically for this purpose. This speedup in turnover, a somewhat earlier retirement, plus heightened expectations of a challenging and profitable later career in civilian life, might also reduce political friction between the civilian and military sectors which tends to produce a political climate hardly conducive to maximum development. Perhaps one way of breaking the introduction of the military and political cycles outlined at the beginning of this paper is to identify the two so closely that they become one in the sense of a mutual commitment to national development and of an insight into the very real problems inherent in the process. There are no easy answers.

Not making the answers any easier to come by is the almost complete absence of serious research in Western schools of education and elsewhere relating to such matters as:

1. The retention of literacy after a terminal five-year primary education ending at age twelve or thirteen.

2. Development of literature and motivations that might generate a higher level of retention of literacy by young teenagers.

3. The use of educational radio or television systems in circumstances similar to those found in Turkey.

4. The development of a literature appealing to the new, adult, intelligent literate.

5. The feasibility of a compressed, pre-university education beginning in the mid-teens.

6. The materials and methods most effective in giving intelligent adults an accelerated pre-university education.

7. The feasibility of administering a test measuring motivation (or "need achievement") to those for whom higher education facilities will be open.

8. Central control of admission to higher education and the flow of students into subject area without impinging on academic freedom.

9. The optimum level of proficiency to be required of graduates of professional schools in Turkey. (One suspects, for example, that Western standards in such fields of medicine may not be appropriate.)

10. The social-psychological effect on intelligent adult illiterates of acquiring literacy.

11. The feasibility of breaking down some jobs requiring high-level manpower into jobs of lesser scope requiring less training (e.g., in medicine, the training of more midwives, inoculators, first aid corpsmen, bonesetters, etc., in place of the medical doctor).

What makes the Turkish case so significant is the awareness of many of Turkey's educational policy makers and administrators of the need to devise new approaches in order to derive maximum return on educational investment. We may learn much by watching the educational innovations introduced in Turkey, innovations supported on the very highest levels. Cevdet Sunay, President of Turkey, recently proclaimed unequivocally, "The most important people in this country are the teachers. The country will progress because of [them]."

BIBLIOGRAPHY
NOTES

BIBLIOGRAPHY

Abadan, Nermin. *Batĭ Almanyadakĭ Türk İşçileri ve Sorunlarĭ*. Ankara: Başkanlĭk Devlet Matbaasĭ, 1964.

Alexander, Alex P. "Industrial Entrepreneurship in Turkey: Origins and Growth," n.p., 1957 (?). (Typewritten.)

Aral, Namĭk Zeki. "Zirai Coğrafyamĭz," *Türkiye İktisat Gazetesi*, September 9, 1965.

Atok, Oğuz Kâzim. "Ordu ve Köy," *Cumhuriyet*, February 15, 1965.

Bradburn, N. M. "The Managerial Role in Turkey: A Psychological Study." Unpublished Ph.D. dissertation, Harvard University, 1960.

Cannon, Colonel. "Literacy Training in the Turkish Armed Forces." Ankara: Joint American Military Aid Mission to Turkey, 1962. (Typewritten.)

Coombs, Philip H. *Education and Foreign Aid*. Cambridge: Harvard University Press, 1965.

Dodds, C. H. "The Social and Educational Background of Turkish Officials," *Middle Eastern Affairs*, vol. I, no. 3 (June 1965).

Eastmond, Jefferson N. "A Comparison of Education in Turkey and the U.S.A." Ankara: Ministry of Education, 1964. (Mimeographed.)

———— "Educational Attainment in Turkey." Ankara: Ministry of Education, 1964. (Mimeographed.)

———— "School Finance in Turkey." Ankara: Ministry of Education, 1964. (Mimeographed.)

Eldridge, Robert H. "Turkish Emigration to Western Europe: Its Background, Development, and Importance to the Turkish Economy." Unpublished Master's thesis, Massachusetts Institute of Technology, 1966.

Enginsoy, Cemalettin. In *Military Civic Action Programs*. Ankara: Central Treaty Organization, 1964.

"Enlisted Men Specialist and Troop NCO Courses Program for 1964–1965. Ankara: Ministry of National Defense, 1964. (Mimeographed.)

Erder, Negat. "Forecasting Occupational Structure of the Turkish Labour Force." In *Planning Education for Economic and Social Development*. Paris: OECD Mediterranean Regional Project, 1963.

First Five-Year Development Plan, 1963–1967. Ankara: Union of

Chambers of Commerce, Industry and Commodity Exchanges of Turkey, 1963.

Goodman, Neville. "Turkey's Experiment in Socialized Medicine," *The Lancet*, January 4, 1964.

Göksel, Burhan. "Our National Education Problem and Private School," *Cumhuriyet*, January 3, 1964.

Hagen, Everett E. *On the Theory of Social Change*. Homewood (Ill.): Dorsey Press, 1962.

Harbison, F. and C. A. Myers. *Education, Manpower and Economic Growth: Strategies of Human Resource Development*. New York: McGraw-Hill, 1964.

Helling, George. "Changing Attitudes Toward Occupational Status and Prestige in Turkey." University of Omaha, 1958 (?). (Mimeographed.)

Investment Guide to Turkey. Ankara: Union of Chambers of Commerce, Industry and Commodity Exchanges of Turkey, 1964.

Karagöz, Süleyman. *Program Geliştirmede Rehberlik*. Ankara: Öğretmenï İşbaşïnda Yetiştirme Bürosu, 1965.

———— *Yeni İlkokul Programï Taşlağï ve Ünite Çalïşmalarï*. Ankara: Öğretmenï İşbaşïnda Yetiştirme Bürosu, 1965.

Kazamias, Andreas M. "Education and the Quest for Modernity in Turkey: Origins and Growth." University of Wisconsin, 1965. (Typewritten.)

Kennedy, E. "Training Turkish Youth for Future Scientific Needs," *The OECD Observer*, no. 14 (February 1965).

Kocatopçu, Şahap. "The Role of Management in the Development of Turkish Industry." In *Capital Formation and Investment in Industry*. Istanbul: Economic and Social Studies Conference Board, 1963.

Koç, M. Şukru. "Barzani ve Doğu Üzerine," *Cumhuriyet*, July 31, 1966.

Kodamoğlu, M. Nuri. *Türkiyede Eğitim*. Ankara: Millî Egitim Basïmevi, 1965.

Lerner, Daniel. *The Passing of Traditional Society*. Glencoe (Ill.): Free Press, 1958.

———— and Richard D. Robinson. "Swords and Ploughshares: The Turkish Army as a Modernizing Force," *World Politics*, vol. XIII, no. 1 (October 1960).

Maddison, Angus. "Foreign Skills and Technical Assistance in Economic Development," *The OECD Observer*, no. 22 (June 1966).

Malî Yïlï Bütçe Tasarïsïna Ait Gerekçe 1966. Ankara: Government of Turkey, 1965.

Matthews, A. T. J. *Emergent Turkish Administrators*. Ankara: University of Ankara, 1954.

Mauldin, W. Parker. "Fertility Studies: Knowledge, Attitude, and Practice," *Studies in Family Planning*, no. 7 (1965).

Meslekî ve Teknik Öğretim Müesseseriyle İlgili Rakamlar. Ankara: Ministry of Education, 1961.

Moralï, Süeda. "Sïnïflarda Başarï İhtimalleri," *Cumhuriyet*, May 22, 1965.

National Income of Turkey. Ankara: State Institute of Statistics, 1966.

Orel, Adnan. In *Military Civic Action Programs.* Ankara: Central Treaty Organization, 1964.

Özalp, Reşat. *Türkiyede Meslekî ve Teknik Öğretim.* Ankara: Maarif Basïmeri, 1956.

"Report on Developments in Education During the 1962–63 School Year." Presented to the XXVI Educational Conference, Geneva, July 1963. Ankara: Ministry of Education.

Robinson, Richard D. "An Analysis of Turkish Education." Ankara: IBRD, a working paper for the 1950 Economic Survey Mission to Turkey, 1950.

———— *Developments Respecting Turkey.* 4 vols. New York: American Universities Field Staff, 1954–1957.

———— *The First Turkish Republic: A Case Study in National Development.* Cambridge: Harvard University Press, 1963.

Roos, Noralou P. "Changing Patterns of Turkish Public Administration." Massachusetts Institute of Technology, Department of Political Science, March 1966. (Dittoed.)

———— and Leslie L. Roos, Jr. "Changing Patterns of Turkish Public Administration." Massachusetts Institute of Technology, Department of Political Science, June 1966. (Dittoed.)

Rufi, John J. "Secondary Education in Turkey." Ankara: Ministry of Education, 1952. (Typewritten.)

Sarç Ömer C. "Population Trends in Turkey and Their Economic Consequence." In *Capital Formation and Investment in Industry.* Istanbul: The Economic and Social Studies Conference Board, First Conference, 1963.

Stycos, J. Marjorie. "The Potential Role of Turkish Village Opinion Leaders in a Program of Family Planning," *The Public Opinion Quarterly*, vol. XIX (1965).

Talas, Cahit. "Eğitim Sistemimiz ve Kalkïnma," *Cumhuriyet*, December 7, 1965.

Targets for Education in Europe in 1970. Paris: OECD Policy Conference on Economic Growth and Investment in Education, 1962.

Telli, Metin. "Ordu ve Üretim," *Cumhuriyet*, May 16, 1965.

Turkey. Paris: OECD Education and Development Country Reports, Mediterranean Regional Project, 1965.

————

Aylık Bülten (Monthly Bulletin), published by the Central Bank of Turkey, Ankara.

Cumhuriyet (Republic), non-partisan daily newspaper, Istanbul.

Economic Report, published annually by the Union of Chambers of Commerce, Industry and Commodity Exchanges of Turkey, Ankara.

Genel Nüfus Sayimi. Ankara: Devlet İstatistik Enstitüsü.

İstatistik Yilliği (Statistical Annual), published annually, with some years combined, by the Central Statistical Office, Ankara.

Middle East and African Economist, published monthly, Forest Hills, N.Y.

Monthly Bulletin of Statistics. Ankara: Central Statistical Office.

News from Turkey. New York: Turkish Information Office (published periodically, no longer appearing).

Nüfus Sayimlari (Population Census). Ankara: Central Statistical Office.

Review of Economic Conditions, published bi-monthly by the Turkish Business Bank, Ankara.

Türkiye İktisat Gazetesi, bi-weekly publication of the Union of Chambers of Commerce, Industry and Commodity Exchanges of Turkey, Ankara.

Turkish Economic Review, published bi-monthly by the Union of Chambers of Commerce, Industry and Commodity Exchanges, Ankara.

Umumi Nüfus Sayimi. Ankara: İstatistik Umum Müdürlüğü.

NOTES

CHAPTER I. THE HISTORICAL INPUT

1. *Türkiye İktisat Gazetesi*, June 17, 1965.

CHAPTER II. DIRECTIONS OF SOCIAL CHANGE

1. See *First Five-Year Development Plan, 1963–1967* (Ankara: Union of Chambers of Commerce, Industry and Commodity Exchanges of Turkey, 1963), p. 69.
2. *New York Times*, June 22, 1965.
3. *Five-Year Plan*, p. 66.
4. Former Minister of Health and Social Welfare, Professor Dr. Rağip Üner, as reported in *Cumhuriyet*, January 26, 1965.
5. Report of a study made by the Izmir Chamber of Commerce, *Cumhuriyet*, December 17, 1964.
6. *İstatistik Yıllığı, 1960–62* (Ankara: Central Statistical Office, 1964), p. 70.
7. It has been estimated by Turks that 8.5 million out of 31.0 million total population are either of Kurdish ethnic identity or Shiite religious persuasion, or both. See *Cumhuriyet*, "Kurt Meselesi," May 6, 1966.
8. See Everett E. Hagen, *On the Theory of Social Change* (Homewood [Ill.], 1962).
9. *İstatistik Yıllığı, 1960–62*, pp. 76–77.
10. For development of this thesis, see R. D. Robinson, *The First Turkish Republic: A Case Study in National Development* (Cambridge [Mass.], 1963), pp. 42–43.
11. *İstatistik Yıllığı, 1960–62*, p. 76.
12. Jefferson N. Eastmond, "Educational Attainment in Turkey" (Ankara: Ministry of Education, 1964), p. 21.
13. For example, see Neville M. Goodman, "Turkey's Experiment in Socialized Medicine," *The Lancet*, January 4, 1964, pp. 36–38.
14. Ömer C. Sarç, "Population Trends in Turkey and Their Economic Consequence," in *Capital Formation and Investment in Industry* (Istanbul: The Economic and Social Studies Conference Board, 1963), p. 61.

CHAPTER III. DIRECTIONS OF ECONOMIC CHANGE

1. İstatistik Yıllığı, 1960–62, p. 432; National Income of Turkey (Ankara: State Institute of Statistics, 1966).
2. Five-Year Plan, p. 25.
3. F. Harbison and C. A. Myers, Education, Manpower and Economic Growth (New York, 1964), pp. 31–33.
4. Price data calculated from Aylık Bülten (Ankara: Central Bank of Turkey, July–December 1960), p. 36; (August 1964), p. 40.
5. Economic Report, 1963 (Ankara: Union of Chambers of Commerce, Industry and Commodity Exchanges of Turkey, 1964), p. 149; Cumhuriyet, January 4, 1965, and January 11, 1965.
6. Economic Report, 1963, p. 150.
7. Five-Year Plan, p. 15; for 1964, see Türkiye İktisat Gazetesi, July 16, 1966, p. 4.
8. Türkiye İktisat Gazetesi, July 10, 1965, p. 3 and July 16, 1966, p. 4.
9. Five-Year Plan, p. 9; Review of Economic Conditions (Ankara: Turkish Business Bank, January–February, 1966), p. 14.
10. Five-Year Plan, p. 23.
11. Jefferson N. Eastmond, "School Finance in Turkey" (Ankara: Ministry of Education, 1964), p. 15.
12. Ibid., p. 11.
13. Ibid.
14. Süeda Moralı, "Sınıflarda Başarı İhtimalleri," Cumhuriyet, May 22, 1965.
15. Eastmond, "School Finance," p. 21.
16. Jefferson N. Eastmond, "A Comparison of Education in Turkey and the U.S.A." (Ankara: Ministry of Education, 1964), p. 11.

CHAPTER IV. HIGH-LEVEL MANPOWER DEMAND

1. Five-Year Plan, pp. 417–19; see also Negat Erder, "Forecasting Occupational Structure of the Turkish Labour Force," in Planning Education for Economic and Social Development (Paris: OECD Mediterranean Regional Project, 1963), pp. 139–146.
2. Angus Maddison, "Foreign Skills and Technical Assistance in Economic Development," The OECD Observer, no. 22 (June 1966), p. 17.
3. Turkey (Paris: OECD Education and Development Country Reports, 1965), pp. 38–40.
4. Five-Year Plan, p. 420.
5. Ibid., p. 42.
6. Ibid., p. 450.
7. İstatistik Yıllığı, 1960–62, pp. 417, 419, 421, 422, 426.

8. "State Statistical Institute," reported in *Cumhuriyet*, March 27, 1965.

CHAPTER V. HIGH-LEVEL MANPOWER SUPPLY

1. *Five-Year Plan*, pp. 418, 425.

2. *Türkiye İktisat Gazetesi*, June 23, 1966, p. 7.

3. Based on a small sample of Turkish workers in Germany in 1963, an analysis showed 49 per cent to be primary school graduates, 15 per cent to be institute or vocational school graduates, 13 per cent to be middle school graduates, and 5 per cent to have graduated from lycée or university. Nermin Abadan, *Batı Almanyadaki Türk İşçileri ve Sorunları* (Ankara, 1964), p. 61. Again, 54 per cent reported prior employment in Turkey as either industrial or transport labor or small craftsmen, an added 16 per cent as administrative, sales, or professional personnel (*ibid.*, p. 17). Presently, the majority of Turkish workers in Germany are earning from $150 to $175 per month gross. Robert H. Eldridge, "Turkish Emigration to Western Europe: Its Background, Development, and Importance to the Turkish Economy" (unpublished Master's thesis, Massachusetts Institute of Technology, 1966), p. 46. Use of his material is by permission of the author.

4. *Five-Year Plan*, pp. 430, 437.

5. *Targets for Education in Europe in 1970* (Paris: OECD Policy Conference on Economic Growth and Investment in Education, 1962), p. 110.

6. See "Enlisted Men Specialist and Troop NCO Courses Program for 1964–65" (Ankara: Ministry of National Defense, 1964).

7. "Report on Developments in Education During the 1962–63 School Year," presented to the XXVI Educational Conference, Geneva, July 1963 (Ankara: Ministry of Education), pp. 6–7.

8. *Five-Year Plan*, p. 427.

9. General Cevdet Sunay in *Cumhuriyet*, December 3, 1964.

CHAPTER VI. THE PROCESS OF HUMAN CAPITAL FORMATION

1. Official report in *Cumhuriyet*, February 27, 1964.

2. Former Minister of Education Dr. İbrahim Öktem in *Cumhuriyet*, September 17, 1964.

3. *Cumhuriyet*, July 16, 1964.

4. *İstatistik Yıllığı, 1960–62*, p. 141.

5. Colonel Cannon, "Literacy Training in the Turkish Armed Forces" (Ankara: Joint American Military Aid Mission to Turkey, 1962).

6. *Five-Year Plan*, p. 424.

7. N. M. Bradburn, "The Managerial Role in Turkey: A Psycho-

logical Study" (unpublished Ph.D. dissertation, Harvard University 1960), p. 139.

8. *Ibid.*, pp. 141–42.

9. Süleyman Karagöz, *Yeni İlkokul Programĭ Taşlağĭ ve Ünite Çalĭşmalarĭ* (Ankara: Öğretmenĭ İşbaşĭnda Yetiştirme Bürosu, 1965); see also S. Karagöz, *Program Geliştirmede Rehberlik* (Ankara: Öğretmenĭ İşbaşĭnda Yetiştirme Bürosu, 1965).

10. Announcement by the Minister of Education, Orhan Dengiz. *Cumhuriyet*, January 1, 1966. See also *Cumhuriyet*, May 18, 1967.

11. Burhan Göksel, "Our National Education Problem and Private School," *Cumhuriyet*, January 3, 1964.

12. Andreas M. Kazamias, "Education and the Quest for Modernity in Turkey: Origins and Growth" (University of Wisconsin, 1965), Table 12, p. 328. Field work done in 1962–63.

13. *New York Times*, October 21, 1963.

14. *İstatistik Yĭllĭğĭ, 1960–62*, p. 173.

15. Daniel Lerner, *The Passing of Traditional Society* (Glencoe [Ill.], 1958).

16. See Daniel Lerner and Richard D. Robinson, "Swords and Ploughshares: The Turkish Army as a Modernizing Force," World Politics, vol. XIII, no. 1 (October 1960), p. 19.

17. Major General Cemalettin Enginsoy in *Military Civic Action Programs* (Ankara: Central Treaty Organization, 1964), pp. 63–64.

18. Brigadier General Adnan Orel, *ibid.*, pp. 67–68; see also Oğuz Kâzim Atok, "Ordu ve Köy," *Cumhuriyet*, February 15, 1965.

19. *Cumhuriyet*, December 27, 1964.

20. Orel, *Military Civic Action Programs*, note 66 on p. 71.

21. Metin Telli, "Ordu ve Üretim," *Cumhuriyet*, May 16, 1965.

22. The Turkish Minister of Health recently estimated the number of Turkish doctors practicing abroad to lie between 2,500 and 3,000. *Cumhuriyet*, January 10, 1965.

23. Abadan, *Batĭ Almanyadakĭ*, p. 67.

24. *Ibid.*, p. 47.

25. *Ibid.*, p. 50.

26. For details of the Turkish emigrant labor program, I am greatly indebted to Robert H. Eldridge ("Turkish Emigration").

27. *Turkish Economic Review*, vol. v, nos. 4 and 5 (July–August 1964), p. 15.

28. Eldridge, "Turkish Emigration," based on a letter from Professor Dr. Yĭlmaz Altuğ to Eldridge, dated April 12, 1966.

29. *Turkish Economic Review*, vol. VI, nos. 6 and 7 (September–October 1965), p. 25.

30. *Ibid.*, vol. V, nos. 8 and 9 (November–December, 1964), pp. 7 and 18.

CHAPTER VII. THE PROCESS OF ALLOCATION

1. George Helling, "Changing Attitudes Toward Occupational Status and Prestige in Turkey" (University of Omaha, 1958 [?]), pp. 2–3.
2. *Ibid.*, p. 8.
3. Kazamias, "Education and the Quest for Modernity," p. 285.
4. Noralou P. Roos and Leslie L. Roos, Jr., "Changing Patterns of Turkish Public Administration" (Massachusetts Institute of Technology, Department of Political Science, March 1966), p. 5.
5. Noralou P. Roos, "Changing Patterns of Turkish Administration" (Massachusetts Institute of Technology, Department of Political Science, March 1966), p. 5.
6. Reanalysis by N. P. Roos, "Changing Patterns," of data from a study by J. Marjorie Stycos, "The Potential Role of Turkish Village Opinion Leaders in a Program of Family Planning," *The Public Opinion Quarterly*, vol. XIX (1965), pp. 120–30.
7. A. T. J. Matthews, *Emergent Turkish Administrators* (Ankara, 1954), p. 24.
8. Reported verbally by Leslie L. Roos, Jr. (Massachusetts Institute of Technology, 1967).
9. Alex P. Alexander, "Industrial Entrepreneurship in Turkey: Origins and Growth" (n.p., 1957 [?]).
10. Şahap Kocatopçu, "The Role of Management in the Development of Turkish Industry," in *Capital Formation and Investment in Industry* (Istanbul: Economic and Social Studies Conference Board, 1963), p. 55.
11. *Ibid.*
12. C. H. Dodds, "The Social and Educational Background of Turkish Officials," *Middle Eastern Affairs*, vol. I, no. 3 (June 1965), p. 27.
13. Roos and Roos, "Changing Patterns," p. 11.
14. Noralou Roos, "Changing Patterns," p. 16.
15. *Cumhuriyet*, May 11, 1967.

CHAPTER VIII. POLICY IMPLICATIONS AND CONCLUSIONS

1. *İstatistik Yıllığı, 1960–62*, pp. 169–171.
2. See John J. Rufi, "Secondary Education in Turkey" (Ankara: Ministry of Education, 1952).
3. E. Kennedy, "Training Turkish Youth for Future Scientific Needs," *The OECD Observer*, no. 14 (February 1965), p. 40.
4. *Ibid.*
5. For example, in a published statement Professor Dr. Cahit Talas observes that the educational system is not meeting the needs of a developing economy. He goes on to point out that a long-run university development plan should run parallel to, and in harmony with,

the national development plan. See his "Eğitim Sistemimiz ve Kalkĭnma," *Cumhuriyet,* December 7, 1965.

6. For example, Ömer Celal Sarç's statement before the Budget Commission of the National Assembly, reported in *Cumhuriyet,* December 30, 1964.